Praise for *Busy but Balanced*

"Too busy to read *Busy but Balanced*? Then open Mimi Doe's helpful book at random and glean a quick morsel of wisdom to nourish the spirit . . . in an instant."—Mary Ellen "Angel Scribe," author of *Expect Miracles* and *A Christmas Filled with Miracles*

"Mimi Doe's latest book is an incandescent guide for today's busy, overwhelmed parents—her words shimmer with insights, solace, and life-transforming tips. I couldn't put it down!"—Stacy DeBroff, author of *Mom Central*

"Mimi Doe's compassionate and insightful book provides a healing balm for every overburdened parent. Instead of adding to our guilt with unattainable visions of the perfect family, her practical tips help us achieve a more attainable goal: transforming family life from frenetic-and-frazzled to busy-but-balanced. By reconnecting our everyday world of chores and schedules to the world of spirit, Mimi reminds us that parenting is sacred work."—Robert Gerzon, author of *Finding Serenity in the Age of Anxiety*

"The difference between dreaming of a more serene life with children and actually having such a life lies in practical, everyday actions. Mimi Doe's *Busy but Balanced* is filled with wonderful ideas, tips, and inspirational thoughts. She takes peaceful parenting from the realm of philosophy and puts it into practical application. Every parent can benefit from her loving suggestions. I will be putting this book on my list of recommended resources." —William Martin, author of *The Parent's Tao Te Ching*

"In *Busy but Balanced*, Mimi Doe has ingeniously compiled a delectable buffet of creative and simple ways for parents and children to relate to each other more authentically and experience a profound increase in quality family time. Step by step, this guidebook helps parents achieve day-to-day peace and fulfillment in their family life, capitalizing on love, support for individuality, and fun. This book is the perfect answer to the prayers of stressed-out, overwhelmed moms and dads."—Gail McMeekin, author of *The Power of Positive Choices* and *The 12 Secrets of Highly Creative Women*

"I love this book! It's beautifully written and brimming with wisdom. If you want to create a healthy, balanced, and spiritual family life, put yourself into Mimi Doe's wonderfully capable hands. In a time when frantic, overly busy lives seem to be the norm, she points the way to an oasis of sanity and calm."
—Lynn A. Robinson, author of *Divine Intuition*

"In this beautifully structured parenting guide, Mimi Doe has written another remarkable book of accessible, spiritual, and, most of all, joyful advice applicable not only to those we hold dearest, but also ourselves. She urges us to open our hearts and practice mindful parenting in ways that easily integrate into daily life. Mimi lets us have it all. We can remain busy but also achieve balance."—Celia Straus, author of *Prayers on My Pillow*

BUSY
BUT
BALANCED

BUSY
BUT
BALANCED

Practical and

Inspirational Ways

to Create a Calmer,

Closer Family

Mimi Doe

ST. MARTIN'S GRIFFIN NEW YORK

BUSY BUT BALANCED. Copyright © 2001 by Mimi Doe. All rights reserved.
Printed in the United States of America. No part of this book may be used or
reproduced in any manner whatsover without written permission except in the
case of brief quotations embodied in critical articles or reviews. For information, address St. Martin's Press, 175 Fifth Avenue, New York, N.Y. 10010.

www.stmartins.com

Book design by Donna Sinisgalli

Library of Congress Cataloging-in-Publication Data

Doe, Mimi.
    Busy but balanced : practical and inspirational ways to create a calmer,
closer family / Mimi Doe.
        p. cm.
    Includes bibliographical references.
    ISBN 0-312-27221-9
    1. Parenting.   2. Parenting—Religious aspects.   3. Child rearing.
4. Child rearing—Religious aspects.   I. Title.

HQ755.8 .D64 2001
649'1—dc21   2001041012

First Edition: December 2001

10 9 8 7 6 5 4 3 2 1

Contents

INTRODUCTION:
SEIZE THE DAY—CALMLY

Often when I give a workshop or talk, parents rush to tell me how inspired they are at the idea of nurturing their children's spiritual lives but wonder how they can possibly do so between managing busy work schedules, kids' sports practices, homework, appointments, cooking healthy meals, and just getting through each day. They want to experience a more peaceful life, raise kind, honorable children, accomplish a personal goal or reach a dream, while being a committed parent—but how?

I, too, struggle with this balance, as I attempt to be a nurturing mother to my two children, a caring partner to my husband, a force of good in my community, and someone who makes a difference through my work. I want to live a vibrant, creative, full life that keeps me busy, but I want that balanced with cozy family time, spiritual growth, laughter, and renewal.

I'm sure you feel this pull. Your days are jammed. You are living a life very much *of* this world. Perhaps you are struggling with how to balance work and family. Maybe getting the dishes done, the dog walked, the VCR fixed, bills paid, notes written, shirts dry-cleaned, dents repaired, armpits deodorized, hedges clipped, memos typed, calories counted, magazines thrown out, and baby books filled are dimming your dreams. Rather than coming to a grinding halt, taking a sabbatical, and chanting in the woods for weeks, you *can* create harmony within your everyday life. Indeed, this is the grace called balance. It is what allows you to savor your family and enjoy your life instead of breathlessly marching through it.

It's okay to be busy! But are we scheduling our lives or living them? Are we present to enjoy the days we create? Will we be able to look back and say that we loved being a parent? We choose how to manage our hours. We are always allowed to say no. The goal is to have the reserves, structure, and balance in place to be able to say yes! to the opportunities that give us joy.

Somehow we have been tricked into believing we can't have it all. We think that success comes at the expense of our family and that failure is a result of not having worked hard enough. The truth is that success comes to those who have created a balance between striving and serenity, effort and yielding. The most successful, happy people I know are pursuing their heart's desire while maintaining equilibrium in their lives.

Relationships, career, physical activity, soulful growth, home, money, and parenting are all entwined. When one area is atrophied or overstimulated, we feel exhausted, anxious, unhappy, lost, empty, or afraid. When we wake up feeling calm, hopeful, and eager for our day to unfold, chances are our lives are flowing with balance. When you're in the current of a balanced life, everything seems to work. You manifest quickly, your intuition guides you clearly, your family life runs smoothly, you feel alive, patient, and vital—there is enough of you to go around. Getting the energy flowing in all areas of your life is a magnificent experience. It's heaven on earth and it's possible for you.

Of course complete balance every day is an unreachable reality, particularly while raising our children. Flexibility is important. What works today may be out of sync tomorrow. The key is to remain open to new solutions and aware when the flags of imbalance begin to wave in your household—resentment, fatigue, depression, whining kids, cranky adults, unexplained tummy aches.

We also need to consider the rhythm of our entire lives. In other words, you might not travel on exotic vacations, dance naked in the moonlight at midnight, or hike the entire Appalachian Trail when you have a baby. You *can,* however, experience the essence of those experiences that balance you: spend a day alone doing something you love, dance with the baby in the backyard, or hike local conservation land, while continuing to plan lifelong goals and dreams.

In my research (working with hundreds of people in workshop settings), the two leading causes of regret in people's lives are inaction—failing to seize the day—and a family life that feels out of control. The busyness of their lives, the small tasks and many distractions, have consistently taken precedence over embracing the day with action toward positive life goals as well as embracing those they love with an authentic awareness.

A lack of presentness colors most of our lives. We are managing our children instead of enjoying their companionship. We are getting ahead in our jobs rather than relishing what we do each day. We seem to be running a race we didn't realize we signed up for, with no finish line in sight.

Many of us don't make the space in our lives to pause and examine; we just don't have that kind of time. If we do manage to slow down and probe, we might only skim the surface and touch on our current problems or material desires. Sometimes examining our lives requires too much follow-up and we feel overwhelmed by the prospect. I'm going to ask you to do some probing throughout *Busy but Balanced,* but the follow-up will be in manageable, realistic, weekly doses.

I believe you have the potential to live a balanced, alive, joy-filled life. You *can* make a difference in your children's futures, manifest your own dreams, and create a soulful home. When you scan your life, take the time to ponder what you see, and generate a plan, you have a vital blueprint to follow. More energy and serendipitous events will follow as a result. It just works that way. You *will* experience a positive shift. Your family can't help but benefit as this grace radiates to them. They will, in turn, begin creating their own blueprints for fulfilling lives and be sustained at home as they move these dreams into action.

The ideas in *Busy but Balanced* are for the people who need them the most—those of us out in the world putting our longings, goals, and ideas into action and balancing that with creating a nourishing home and deeply connecting with our children. It's not about giving up desire but, instead, creating a right relationship with all aspects of ourselves and our world. Rather than breathlessly grasping at the shards of our lives, we can boldly and calmly expand to embrace all aspects of it—alert and relaxed.

A mother of two young children expressed what many of us feel: "I want a simple life; I want a busy life. I don't want it cluttered with junk, but I want it vibrant. My relationship is with my family, and I want that at the core of my life; but I also want meaningful work. My family is forever so I want that to thrive, but I want the day in and day out at work to be good too."

Fear of change locks many of us into rote living—treadmill days. *Busy but Balanced* will help you take action month by month, manage change, even invite it in, to create a full life lived with no regrets. Making choices allows you to live sanely with more joy, energy, and success—without sacrifice.

The stories and ideas in *Busy but Balanced* are meant to help you create a family life rich with meaning in the clutch of the every day. It is my hope that you come to believe that families are created rather than inherited, and you begin to invent yours with imagination and joy. Creating a life you love means putting your own self-care into the equation.

Creating a calmer, more connected family begins with honoring your own mind, body, and spirit—fueling yourself so you can nurture your most important relationships.

Once you commit to creating more balance in your life and a unified family—you have taken a big step by beginning this book—you will find doors opening and events occurring to assist you. I have seen parents who frantically rushed through their days experience a transformation by using some of my "Balancing Tips." You can too!

HOW TO USE THIS BOOK

Busy but Balanced is a year-long balance guide. The seasonal structure made sense to me, given that my life seems to be in rhythm with the seasons, the school calendar, and holidays. Please don't feel locked in by this structure, but rather move through the book in a way that works for you.

Monthly

Each month begins with a list of ideas to help you create a deeper connection with your family or a quiz for insight into your current state of balance. Then there are thoughts that are meant to be digested by themselves. Perhaps you could read a thought per week; or if you have a particular issue at hand, refer to the appropriate thought.

Balancing Tips

The Balancing Tips are a buffet of ideas for you to try. The point isn't to add more tasks to your already full list of "to do's"—that would teeter you over the edge—rather to give you many options with the hope that some of them will spark your interest and trigger your own creative ideas. If you try one tip a week, or take one easy step, you'll begin to see a change in your life.

Resources

At the end of each season is a list of resources that pertain to the themes presented. If you want to explore a particular topic in a deeper way or need information that makes it easier to take action, these books, Web sites, products, and phone numbers will help. These resources will be updated online at www.SpiritualParenting.com.

Quotes

Many of the quotes you'll find sprinkled throughout the book are from children and parents I've worked with. There's nothing like the wisdom of a child to cut right to the core of an issue and the advice of fellow parents to trigger our own "ah ha" moment.

I've collected the other quotes over the years and call upon them for inspiration frequently.

Get the Most from *Busy but Balanced*

So welcome to the *Busy but Balanced* program. You join many other parents who are committed to creating mindful, fulfilling, exciting lives with their families. You are part of a movement that is embracing a new way of parenting, not limited by old associations or guilt-filled "shoulds" but authentic, vital relationships that feed the spirits of both parent and child. Some additional ideas to support you in this program include:

• First thing in the morning and before falling asleep at night, allow your mind to call up the blueprint or visual image of your ideal balanced life. You will create the details of this plan as you move through the monthly thoughts to follow. Whatever you focus on the most, believe in most strongly, and expect to occur, is what you create in your life.

• Form a parenting group that meets monthly to discuss the thoughts and balancing tips presented in this book. You can also share resources, support each other in the parenting process, hire guest speakers, and occasionally include your children for festive family gatherings.

• Take it slow. It's not possible to change family dynamics or self-care strategies overnight. Begin with small changes: Turn off the radio when you're carpooling and listen to your kids rather than the weather report, sign up for that upcoming lecture on organization, wake up fifteen minutes earlier each morning to savor your cup of tea in quiet before the children arise.

• Buy a journal to write in as you work with this book. The very act of writing can focus your thoughts. Rereading entries later can help you understand patterns as well as vividly ignite memories.

Enjoy your parenting journey and delight in creating a busy but balanced life. You *can* do it—beginning right now!

> *It's not enough to be busy . . . the question is: What are we busy about?*
>
> —THOREAU

PART ONE

WINTER

The winter months—especially if you live in a cold climate—can be a time of loneliness and frustration. We tend to stay indoors as the dark, gray days chip away at our energy. Use this season to grow closer as a family and add light to all aspects of your life.

The thoughts presented in the following months suggest you take the time to go within—pay attention to your thoughts, take a look at the role of guilt in your life, become mindful of the present moment, consider your relationship with money, and renew your own spirit within the rhythm of each jam-packed day.

The Balancing Tips will give you specific ways to take action on the ideas you generate from your inward journey. There will also be ways to approach your kids with an open heart to deepen your family connection. —☙

1

JANUARY

WAYS TO BEGIN AGAIN—AS A FAMILY!

The fresh new year is just the time to dive in and begin balancing your life. Start by reevaluating family priorities and developing a plan to honor those choices. Consciously making decisions about how you connect with those you love is the first and vital step to creating more harmony in your life. Your relationships at home can sustain and ground you and your children.

What follows are ideas for approaching family life from a new perspective:

1. Let go of old definitions you might have of your children and see them as the vast spiritual beings they are today. Be open to knowing your family, day by day, in this new year!
2. Pick one day a month as Family Day. Mark each of them on your calendar and begin planning now for all twelve magical days.
3. Begin the new year with less clutter. Go through your closets and give away clothing you haven't used in a year or more. Ask your kids to do the same—toys, books, and tapes can all be passed along to a shelter for homeless families.
4. Call up that feeling of awe you had when your child was born. This will help you begin the habit of coming from the heart when you speak to your son or daughter.

5. If your family shares a hobby, schedule specific times this year to pursue your interests together. If you haven't yet found a mutual hobby, begin exploring—hiking, biking, skiing, collecting coins, watching old musicals.

6. Remain on the lookout for resources to support your children's dreams. Keep a folder handy for each child that you fill with information about his or her interests—articles, upcoming classes, book titles.

7. Designate the refrigerator as the "heart of the home" and post your prayer requests, words for the day, pictures of your friends and family, and any other meaningful visual reminders of all you and your family hold dear.

8. Put the television in a place that takes some effort to reach instead of allowing it to take center stage in your home.

9. Designate a specific week as Family Care Week. Pick names out of a hat so each person in the family has a secret recipient for daily caring deeds. What a surprise to discover your bed is made, for example, when you get out of your morning shower or the dog is fed on your day to handle the pets.

10. Create a visual image of what you would like your family life to be like in the upcoming year. Find pictures of dream vacations, an organized, beautiful home, festive dinners, symbols of harmony, and glue them on a poster board with a photo of your family in the center. Place it in a prominent spot and enjoy visualizing together.

The object of the New Year is not that we should have a new year. It is that we should have a new soul . . .

—G. K. CHESTERTON

MINDFUL PARENTING

One of the greatest challenges as a parent is remaining mindful. Our lives are full to the brim with obligations, tasks, obstacles, tugs, pulls, necessities, responsibilities, crises—and the list goes on. Just tending to the physical needs of our family can zap us of energy. To remain in the moment and truly listen to our eight year old daughter explain the plot of her current favorite book, for example, is tough. The phone is ringing, the dog is barking to go out, and there's no dinner in sight. It is in this very moment, however, when we can choose serenity or stress—for us and for our child.

Unclench your jaw, take a deep breath, and push the pause button on your life. Look into your child's eyes, take her hands in yours, and breathe in her story. If you need to begin again, ask her to take a deep breath with you and be fully together in this moment. Then move on to dinner, the message that's been left on your answering machine, and the dog who now is barking to be let back in.

Use the "crazy moments" of your life as reminders to pause and breathe deeply. Breathe in peace and breathe out chaos. This habit helps you return to the present, to your life as you are living it. It takes you off autopilot. I'm not going to kid you—it takes a while for this to become second nature. We are so programmed to take care of all the details and then grab a moment or two of quiet in between accomplishments. The benefits of mindful parenting, however, are astounding—fewer tension headaches for you, less whining from your kids, and a greater appreciation of life's simple delights for you all. Unexpected good is now able to flow into this paused place.

BALANCING TIPS

—🌀 Be attentive to the expectations you have for yourself and for each of your children. When I was nursing a newborn, all I could do was focus on caring for that baby. After days of tears and frustration over what I hadn't accomplished, I let go and readjusted my impossible agenda. Unrealistic expectations distort our sense of mindfulness and increase our feelings of guilt.

—🌀 Pay attention to the people around your children, such as care-takers, friends, camp counselors, neighbors. Talk to your kids about these people, then listen carefully to what they say. Help your children become mindful of the energy of others and how it makes them feel.

—🌀 Come up with a habit that can place you squarely in the moment. Perhaps you might try the Buddhist practice of repeating what you are doing while you are doing it. I attempt, for instance, to slow my whirling mind during my morning walk by silently repeating, "Walking, just walking."

—🌀 Turn down the sounds in your home—the volume on the television, the computer, stereos. You'll notice a difference in everyone's mindfulness, as well as more room for conversation.

—🌀 A friend just bought an adorable little house for herself and her young daughter. I had a crystal-clear vision, upon seeing it for the first time, of all she could do to create an inviting space. It struck me that I had been walking through my own home unaware for years. I no longer saw the ugly switch plates, weedy front yard, tattered rug, or wobbly bureau.

Pretend you are seeing your home for the very first time as a detached observer. Ask your kids to join you and take a tour, really noticing the details. Observe what small changes you might make to create a more desirable living space. Our homes are an integral part of how we sustain our spirits. Let's observe them with a renewed, mindful vision.

—☙ If you are recycling an old VCR, make sure to salvage the PAUSE button. Put it in a place it will be seen (on your desk, over the kitchen sink, in a frame on the wall) as a reminder to PAUSE and be present in the moment. If you don't have an actual PAUSE button, ask your child with a flair for art to create one for you—even bold printing on an index card will do.

—☙ Ellen, mother of two, taped a note to the front cover of her daily planner to remind her to remain attentive. It says, "Spend time with my children today as if they are dear visitors who are about to leave, because they are."

> We usually think that parents have to nourish their children, but sometimes the children can bring enlightenment to the parents and help transform them.
>
> —THICH NHAT HANH

GOTTA DITCH THAT GUILT

Sometimes we're so caught up in guilt over what we see as our parental flaws that we lack the luster to take the simplest action—it's easier to keep things as they are. We're exhausted and reading one more idea or tip on how to create more meaning in our family or enhance our child's self-esteem gnaws at our raw spot, and we shut down. We've become cynical. "Yeah right, like my kids would ever agree to candles and story-telling instead of television or Gameboy." We choose guilt over change.

Guilt, I promise, is felt by all of us at some point or another. One mother of four told me, "I feel guilty every day for something. But I'm a woman and a mom, so it's par for the course." We can change this course. We can begin to take care of ourselves as we care for those we love, knowing that ultimately it's best for the entire family.

Some of us beat ourselves up when we vary from our limiting definition of a "good parent." We send our four year old to school wearing a bathing suit instead of undies because there just weren't any clean ones. Then we feel as if we should be punished for our incompetence. We're ruthless with ourselves when maybe we should just buy more underwear.

The truth is, we take on this parenting gig with little preparation. The discrepancies between our expectations and reality are huge. My husband had some notion when our first child was born that he could read the *Wall Street Journal* while serenely rocking our infant. The first day she was home from the hospital, he settled her on his chest and awkwardly opened the newspaper. Ha! It didn't jive with his romantic fatherly picture. He adjusted.

Look at your parenting role as a path to greater spiritual awareness (the ultimate in mind/body multitasking). Mistakes are simply opportunities to evolve a little more. Guilt takes us out of the present moment where our kids live and where we need to see and act clearly and into another zone of past pictures and misplaced inner scolding.

Begin to release the current conditioning our culture seems to wrap us in, which suggests that we must listen and give to our children exclusively, without giving to ourselves. Caring for our children's deepest feelings and desires is important, of course, but doing so without attending to our own wants and needs only fuels our guilt, weariness, and resentment. Relationships flourish, families thrive when both parent and child are nourished.

The following ideas will help you ditch the guilt each time it rears its nasty little head:

BALANCING TIPS

꿈 Rather than feeling guilty that your children are in day care, make sure the day care you select reflects your values and expectations. Always follow your intuition. If you're feeling less then confident about the situation, begin this week researching a new arrangement.

꿈 Don't compare your family to the family next door or the family you grew up in or even the families you see on television. What works for you is uniquely yours. My daughter came home astounded that a friend's mother irons her clothing. Did I feel guilty that in twelve years my daughter has never seen an iron, much less worn ironed jeans? Nah.

꿈 You're the parent and you get to construct your own way of doing things. Anything goes. You can set your own priorities. Serve raw carrot sticks and peanut butter on toast for dinner if you want to—it's three food groups. Pile laundered clothes on any available surface for the kids to put away; at least they are clean. There's no expectation that you can't question, no "right way" to run your household. A friend of mine just had her fourth daughter. Sorting socks was the chore that sent her over the edge. So she bought twenty-five pairs of identical white socks. Her three older girls wear the same size, luckily, and now grab their two socks, which always match, from the clean pile—problem solved.

—☙ Sometimes we feel guilty for not spending enough time with our child or for not giving him everything he wants, so we allow him to do as he pleases. The result is a very unattractive and confused kid who knows he can take advantage of our guilt. Instead of giving him free rein, make an effort to spend more time with him in situations where you are able to be fully attentive. Also, say no and mean it. Don't waver back and forth as guilt tugs at your decision-making ability. Kids deserve clear answers. They want *us,* not expensive things that cause their parents to be anxious and debt ridden. Kids need limits created with love, not a pal who is afraid to say no for a parent. It's fine for children to let us know their needs and wants, and it's key that we balance that with what's best for the whole family.

—☙ Many of us feel guilty for wanting time away from our kids. But it is essential to take care of your own body, mind, and spirit. What soothes your soul? Make an appointment this week to engage in that activity—lunch with a friend, a long, hot soak in the tub, time to read an inspirational book. No kidding, do it now! Just to dodge the guilt, remind yourself you're doing it for your kids. Arrange with your partner, barter with a friend, or hire a baby-sitter so you can indulge in your connection with spirit. My daughter let me off the hook with this one. I wanted to go to a Saturday morning yoga class, but I also really wanted to hang out with my family and eat French toast in our jammies. Whitney said, "Mom, you're much nicer after you do yoga." I went to the class. Take care of yourself so you can take better care of your kids.

—☞ Let go of any past mistakes you've made with your children. Forgive yourself and move forward. Then think about how you want to parent differently this year than in the past. Create a clear picture in your mind. Write down the qualities you'd like to have more of: patience, understanding, joyful acceptance. Keep the list handy to remind yourself of the picture you imagined.

—☞ Put your guilt to good use. If you feel awful over unkind words you said to your child, tell her you're sorry. If you feel you're not spending enough time with your family, reevaluate your schedule. Don't wallow in guilt. Confront it and take action.

—☞ Write your own list of myth busters. Begin with: Parents do lose their tempers, moms don't always want to cuddle, dinner doesn't have to come from a recipe, not every spiritual family goes to church or synagogue each week, calm can be found when dishes aren't done and the house is full of activity.

> *Fear is the tax that conscience pays to guilt.*
> —HOWARD AIKEN

> *Food, love, career, and mothers, the four major guilt groups.*
> —CATHY GUISEWITE

THE MONEY DANCE

A survey was recently conducted by the University of Michigan. They wanted to study what effect money had on people's lives. Three of their findings were: What do people worry about most? Money! What makes people the happiest? Money! What makes people the unhappiest? Money!

Our feelings about the issues of money and prosperity are full and deep and intense and often impenetrable.

One father of three battles his demons with money—demons passed along to him by his father. When he was thirteen years old, his father went bankrupt and lost the farm that had been in the family for generations. As this boy grew up, he had anxiety around money issues and avoided risks of any kind. A woman who is raising two girls on her own was brought up by her grandmother because her own single mother couldn't support them. She lives with the fear of losing her daughters as a result of her unsteady income.

We may not inherit money, but we do inherit an approach to money from our family of origin. Let's take responsibility for our prosperity consciousness, our money mentality, so we can blast away the wall that's keeping abundance from us. When we are alert to our old money programming, we can rewrite the script. Not only will our kids get a healthier example; but by becoming aware of money's role in our own childhood, we can tame negative images and fears. Let's choose, today, to allow and accept all kinds of prosperity into our lives.

I was in my twenties when a friend introduced me to the idea that you can have all you expect and accept. Whatever you visualize as being possible in your life, if you believe, you can achieve. It was an exhilarating realization for me and continues to be a core belief that I rein myself back to understanding. This is a truth I want my children to hinge their lives upon. I have seen how easily life works when I patiently and consistently focus on my dreams and visions. I want that ease for my kids, in their relationship with abundance, and in all areas of their lives.

Money is just energy. If we dare to imagine bounty for ourselves and guide our children to this same mental habit, we will shift our lives in the direction of our dreams. We can write our family's money script and accept and receive prosperity with joy.

Allow the energy of money to flow to you and then lovingly flow back out into the world. Your children are watching.

BALANCING TIPS

Be aware of how you speak about money to your children: "We can't afford this," or, "I'll never have enough." Is there guilt associated with spending? "I've spent a lot of money on your piano lessons so keep practicing."

Give your kids responsibility for using their own money early on. It helps them maintain a balanced perspective on value. My daughter loved special frozen drinks from a local coffee shop. I began to feel the expense wasn't worth the treat and suggested she use her own money. "It's totally not worth $3.50" was her wise response. We concocted our own drink(s) at home.

Take a look at what you might be trading for money—time with your kids, self-nurturing, pursuing a dream. Is there a way you could scale back your expenses to spend time on what you value now?

⟶᧧ Money is a balance buster for many of us. We don't know the best way to manage the money we earn and haven't made the time to learn. Get a grip on family finances by setting up a system for paying bills on time (I like the Quicken software program), saving for college and retirement (automatic savings plans are pure magic), handling debt (find a professional to help you create a plan), and meeting your financial goals (you've got to make these goals before you can meet them). Once you are in control of your money, you won't feel thrown off balance.

⟶᧧ Are you avoiding taking responsibility for money because it elicits feelings of fear, stress, scarcity? Schedule a time each month when you and your partner can review your current financial situation. Create goals and strategies. Is saving for your child's college tuition just a dream? Even if it's an old coffee can for collecting change, just making the dream concrete opens the way for the flow of money.

⟶᧧ Eliminate debt and find exhilarating freedom. Debt can be an anchor around our "financial psyche"—dragging us down in all areas of our lives. Create a debt repayment plan and move on with your life.

> *Prosperity is a way of living and thinking, and not just money or things. Poverty is a way of living and thinking, and not just a lack of money or things.*
>
> —ERIC BUTTERWORTH

PARENTING PRESCRIPTIONS

A prescription may be your validation for doing what otherwise doesn't seem to fit into your life. If the doctor orders bed rest, then you wouldn't

feel guilty tucked in for the allotted time. If the physical ther
a specific round of exercises to strengthen your pulled musc
aside time to do them to ensure a faster recovery.

Think of the following list as prescriptions to be filled when family
spirit is sagging. Write them on index cards and pick one when you need
to prescribe yourself a dose of parenting illumination. A little jolt of
inspiration and imagination in the midst of your busy life can reignite
your passion and send ripples of joy into your family.

- Ask your child to paint a picture of BLISS, then hang it above your
  kitchen table.
- Go outside after dinner with your kids and adopt a star for your
  family. Create its birth certificate using today's date.
- Raise your arms, open your mouth, and shout for joy—in the
  shower, in the car, on the street, in your child's presence. Sure,
  older kids will be mortified to be seen with you, but I guarantee
  they'll remember your exuberance.
- Read a funny poem from one of Shel Silverstein's books aloud at
  breakfast.
- Next Sunday morning play the music that soothes your soul for at
  least ten minutes.
- Light three purple candles for your child's bath tonight—use no
  other lighting.
- Tuck a honey stick in your child's lunch box or backpack tomorrow morning with a little note that begins: "Honey for my honey
  because . . ."
- Set your watch alarm to ring every hour on the hour today; and
  when it does, take a deep breath and smile—regardless of what's
  happening around you.
- Brew up a pot of tea when you reconnect with your child at the

end of the day. Pour a cup for each of you in special mugs or china tea cups. Sit at the kitchen table and listen to your child until your cups are empty.

- Buy a bouquet of flowers on the way home from work and sneak them into your child's room.
- Plan a musical. Invite your children's friends over three Sundays from now for an afternoon of music and fun. Find any musical instruments you have, ask the kids to bring their own, and take turns playing for one another. Invite parents to arrive an hour later for a performance.
- Browse a bookstore's humor section and select the funniest book you can find to share with your family; cartoons or joke books are great. Leave the book in the kitchen and anytime you need a good shot of family laughter or to diffuse tension, ask someone to read a section aloud.
- Pamper yourself: schedule a massage, movie, lunch with a friend. Whatever makes you feel fantastic and cared for is your prescription today.
- Look deeply into your child's eyes right now. Pause in whatever you are doing and grab that sweet soul by the shoulders, spin him around, and tell him how very much you adore him, whether he is two or twenty-two.
- Tie a ribbon around the kitchen faucet as a gratitude reminder. Each time you see it, pause and allow feelings of deep thanks to wash over you. Give thanks for your beautiful child, your ability to move one step closer to your ideal life, the gifts of more power, clarity and vision today, the gentle wind that blows through the window.
- Find the nearest miniature or crazy golf course. Leave your work and your worries at home. Load up the kids, their friends, anyone

who happens to be within ten feet of the car, and play a wacky round.

• Rent an old musical and watch it with your kids this Friday night. Pop some popcorn and sing along.

• Slip a heating pad, hot water bottle, or microwavable heat pillow, into your child's chilly bed before he or she climbs in. Talk about the warming pans and hot potatoes that were used to warm beds in the olden days. When your child is asleep, retrieve the heat pillow, warm it up, and wrap it around your neck. Feel any stress ease right away.

• Buy a little pot of face glitter and come down to breakfast with it sprinkled on your cheeks. Apply a dab to your child's face, anointing her part of the "glitter family." Tell her you are connected to each other by sparkles as you set out to explore your magical day.

My mom can surprise me right out of a bad mood.

—AGE 8

LETTING GO OF FEAR AND DOUBT

Fear prevents us from moving forward with joy. It knocks us off balance, causing us to tighten our grip on the positive motion of our lives.

Fear for our children can color our choices, reactions, and intentions. We worry that our kids might fall behind, underachieve, get hurt, be unfairly judged.

But our fear often becomes our children's fear. Our worry can cause our kids to lose their trust in positive outcomes. In attempting to shield our children from pain, we sometimes block their connection to the magnificent spirit that spontaneously pours through them.

Apprehension shuts out our ability to hear the constant guidance that is always available. Let's shift from fear to trust by coming up with a mental trigger—a switch to flip—when we are about to enter the doubt zone. Close your eyes and picture a giant light switch—red and blinking. Now pretend you are flipping the switch off, the blinking stops; this is your signal to release fear and calmly trust in Divine order. Make it a habit, when fear creeps into your consciousness, to flip that mental switch.

It's easier to follow our guidance as earthly escorts for our kids when our fear is under control. Our children are dancing their own life dance, guided by their spirits, and it's our jobs to joyfully facilitate that dance rather than trip them up with our unnecessary worry. Everything changes, especially our kids. Rather than fear their growth, embrace it. See your children move down their life paths full of Divine guidance and love.

It's tough, as a parent, to resign as general manager of the universe. Peace comes, however, when we release our worries and know our children are lovingly guided. Tranquility is always available within. Let's model ways for our kids to access it and ground ourselves in this inner pool of refreshing calm.

B A L A N C I N G   T I P S

⟿ Focusing on fears and visualizing dreaded outcomes can manifest exactly what you don't want. Instead, each time you begin to picture a negative scenario, erase the blackboard of your mind or put a red slash through the mental picture. Now, picture what you'd like to occur.

—☙   Rather than believe that each choice is final and unalterable, lighten up and realize your role as a parent is that of a loving guide. Try this affirmation: "My decisions are made by following my deepest intuition; I let go of fear and trust that all is well; I do the best I can, drawing the right information and ideas to me."

—☙   Take a look at the rules and regulations you've created for your kids. Are any of them made out of fear or distrust? Restricting our children because of our own fears can curb their creativity, self-expression, and freedom to take risks.

—☙   This also applies to our schedules. Are we running our kids ragged with perpetual motion? Could this be because we are afraid of their falling behind or not living up to their potential? Examine the reasons behind your calendar. Might there be a small fear of slowing down and really examining your life?

—☙   Trust yourself and your deepest knowing about your kids. Shelia has used her fear to move forward into trusting herself as a parent: "I never felt so much fear until I became a parent. I didn't want anything bad to happen to this helpless being that I was put in charge of. My first experience with parenting was black and white, there was a right way and a wrong way to do things. I empowered myself with knowledge. The more I read, I saw that three well-known and respected pediatricians all had the right but different answers. I slowly learned to read the advice of these doctors and listen to my own pediatrician, but I also learned to read my child. When this happened a whole new world opened up. We began to bond and communicate as only a mother and child can. As a mother you just know things about your child. I live with everyday fear by turning it over to God."

—ↄ Get a grip on control issues. We often react to fear by holding even tighter to those things we can control in our lives. Stress and anxiety surface when we try to control the uncontrollable. We can't change the weather, our child's tummy bug, or someone else's behavior. What is good and bad control? Bad control can knock us off balance and good control can move us forward into living our dreams. Examine when you try to control the uncontrollable and think about how you can ease up. Take charge of those aspects in your life where you do hold the reins.

> *I think I must let go. Must fear not, must be quiet*
> *so that my children can hear the Sound of Creation*
> *and dance the dance that is in them.*
>
> —RUSSELL HOBAN

PITCHING IN

Time experts, organization gurus, and life coaches all say the same thing about creating more order in our lives: delegate. But to whom, I scream from my spot on the other side of the page, do I delegate? Hire someone to do the "stuff" you don't want to do, they say. Again, I toss down the magazine or book and wonder how most of us can afford to hire out the never-ending list of chores that come from living in busy households. My army of workers consists of two little girls, one dog, one cat, and a more than willing but also short on time husband.

When my children were younger, I would put on a trench coat, collar up, grab a notepad, and take on a mysterious accent. "The room inspector is here," I would command. "Time for a room check." The girls would stop whatever they were doing and gleefully dash to their rooms to tidy up before the room inspector arrived. The room inspector even made guest appearances to exasperated friends' homes upon occasion.

Sadly, the kids have outgrown the room inspector. I want them to have pride in their home, however, and to participate as active members of the family. It's also high on my list to rid the house of damp towels dropped along the route from bathroom to bedrooms.

I'd like my kids to understand how a clean home frees their minds from distraction and allows them to connect to their creativity and intuition. Clearing the clutter is a modern-day alchemy and can transform our lives, but how can I motivate my family to dive in with gusto so they can experience the powerful flow of life energy?

I decided to ask my workshop participants and newsletter subscribers for their advice. "How do your children help around the house?" Their creative ideas have helped jump-start the chore issue in my household. Rather than nagging for some simple help, chores have become kind of interesting around here. Oh, and I've put a hook on the bathroom door for those wet towels.

Here are some of their suggestions:

B A L A N C I N G   T I P S

— "I invented the 'wheel of housework' for my ten year old. I made a spinner, like those on board games, and put all the different areas of the house on it. Whichever room it lands on, we tidy up."

— "Last year I came up with the idea that both the girls and boys could plan one dinner a month. It has been great and provided some

interesting meals. Not everything has to be homemade, you can buy
pesto at the grocery!"

—◌ "I tape money to the bottom of all my wastebaskets. When the
children empty one, they get the coin. In a few days I replace the
money. It's like a treasure hunt. I sometimes tape candy (wrapped) to
the window cleaner and furniture spray. The children dust and do mirrors now with excitement."

—◌ "Nothing works better than the chore jar. At the beginning of
the week, I write the chores that need to be done on bits of paper
and put them into a special jar that the kids have decorated. They are
small tasks so that my younger kids can do them, with the older ones
picking more than one slip of paper. For example, empty the dishwasher,
take out the trash, clear the table, put dishes in the dishwasher, feed the
animals. Larger tasks such as wash the car or put away laundry are listed
twice so two kids will share the task. It has become a fun tradition to
draw a chore and there is much less complaining."

—◌ "When kids leave their toys and clothing lying around our house,
the offending items go to jail. I put a note in the child's room saying,
'Help, I'm your red clog and I'm in jail.' The child then has the choice
of letting it serve out its time (a few days) or bailing it out by doing a
chore of my choice."

—◌ "My husband and I used to make a list of chores to be done when
we went out for the evening. The kids signed up and did them while we
were gone. When we got home, they were proud they had done the
chores by themselves without us around to check up on the progress.

This worked until adolescence, and then nothing we did worked well! I gave up trying to get them to keep their rooms clean at this time and decided, as long as nothing crawled out on legs or grew green mold, their rooms were their own and I simply asked that they keep their doors closed. It was very hard for me to do this since I like a neat house, but I did not want to have a power struggle over *things,* thereby possibly encouraging resentment and lack of communication on the really important issues like drugs, sex, etc. Three out of four children today are 'neat' people and cannot stand to be in messy homes."

—◡ "I hated the weekly nagging on cleaning up rooms, so I let the kids pick one day of the week when they do their work. Now, no more nagging! Sometimes the mess in between drives me crazy, but I feel better knowing that on 'their' day it will be picked up!"

2

FEBRUARY

FAMILY LOVE— VALENTINE'S DAY AND BEYOND!

Valentine's Day isn't just for romantic love. Of course we all still want to be romanced, but consider marking Valentine's Day as an occasion to remind your kids that they are cherished and to spread love around *all* areas of your life.

1. Make a list of the qualities you love in your child. Type it on decorated paper, roll it up, and tie it with festive ribbons. Place this love scroll on his breakfast plate to find first thing Valentine's morning.

2. Come up with a secret way to show love to someone you know doesn't receive much. How about heart-shaped muffins in a pretty basket left on an elderly neighbor's doorstep?

3. Ask your kids what's beautiful to them; then include more of it in their lives.

4. Have a family Valentine's dinner—lots of red candles, lacy doilies, little white lights wrapped around the room, and heartfelt conversation.

5. Don't forget to care for your own well-being—more sleep, healthy foods, time alone, laughing with friends. It's easier to be loving parents when we love ourselves.

6. Tell your kids the feelings you had when you saw each one of them for the first time—the amazing love that washed over you. They'll want to hear this love story again and again.

7. Come up with a secret sign that means "I love you." It comes in handy at the bus stop or in a crowded room.

8. In addition to the expected chocolates, give your child the gift of your time. A heart-shaped note could list ideas such as: a hike together, breakfast on Saturday morning (you choose where), your favorite book (read by me).

9. Take a close look at your daily activities. Could you focus more on caring for each other than caring for things?

10. Remind your kids that real love doesn't expect a payback.

COLLECTIONS, TREASURES, AND CREATIONS

There's something about aspects of the simplicity movement that leave me a little cold. Sure I crave order in my home. I grapple with the clutter of a busy family life. When everything has a place, I feel more peaceful; and when my home's been cleaned, I experience a spiritual renewal that brings a chorus of Alleluia's to my lips.

But within that order there needs to be a space for the mementos that support the souls of those of us living here—objects with a story, creations made by small hands, treasures found in nature, collections gathered over time, photographs that ignite memories. By honoring what is meaningful to us, we create a home that sustains our family and shelters us during the difficult times.

My friend Janice, mother of three, finds a connection to her childhood through her kitchen collection: "We have a huge collection of cooking items because the kids and I cook together—old bowls of my mother's, my grandmother's meat grinder, the butter churn from my father's boyhood farm. We use and display these treasures. Our kitchen is cramped, but it feels good to be in the space with these meaningful things."

One family I know built an entire room onto their home as a dedicated display center, a minimuseum for their children's treasures and hobbies. They hauled home whale bones they found on the beach and reassembled the skeleton in this room. Most of us are lucky if we can clear off a shelf for our children to display their finds. My family has dedicated the kitchen windowsill as our lucky rock display center. We've been collecting shiny black rocks with mystical white lines that wrap around them from our summer trips to Maine.

Simplicity is important, but let's not disregard the essence of our souls. May the following ideas ignite your household vision:

BALANCING TIPS

⟶ Hang family pictures in groupings. Invite your family history into your everyday lives.

⟶ Create a seasonal nature table adorned with found objects, such as feathers, abandoned birds' nests, driftwood, dried flowers, nut shells, sea glass.

⟶ Have your children thread large, dried seeds (sunflower or melon work nicely) onto thick string and use them as curtain tiebacks or garlands around a doorway.

⟶ Allow gourds, pumpkins, and squashes to dry out; then varnish them with shellac. Their beautiful natural colors add depth to a bare corner of any room.

⟶ The mantelpiece has become a classic domestic shrine for many family homes, but don't forget other spots to display sacred objects both found and purchased as well as those created by family members or handed down. Windowsills, shelves, bare corners, occasional tables, landings, stair corners, even a cardboard box with a pretty cloth all offer interesting space for meaningful objects to perch on.

I have been collecting pitchers since I was two years old and spent all day pouring water back and forth, back and forth from pitcher to pitcher.

All my pitchers are lined up on a shelf I see
every time I go downstairs to play.

—AGE 8

THE LOVING POWER OF PETS

I grew up with parents who were animal lovers and advocates. Our lives were full of the usual cats, dogs, and horses, but I'll always remember the winter my mother rescued haggard animals from a local petting zoo. We nurtured a skinny monkey, goats, sheep, deer, even an adolescent armadillo.

Pets were an integral part of our family and their well-being was always considered. My parents went so far as to build a carpeted ramp for an aging cat who could no longer jump on their bed.

My father died at home two years ago with George, their standard poodle, at his side. As Dad's spirit began to leave his body, he called out a warm greeting to Gyp, his beloved Arabian stallion, who appeared to guide him from earth to the beyond, where I'm sure he is now reunited with all of his animal friends.

My life with animals today is much simpler than that of my childhood. We have one cat and one dog, who provide my children with ample companionship and love. The girls rush home to embrace their pets, who eagerly watch for them out the windows. My daughter once told me that her cat knows all her secrets, and her sister misses her dog as much as her family when she goes to a sleepover. (I can't believe I've succumbed to allowing that dog to be her bunk mate.)

Children are attracted to animals because they are unambiguous and honest; animals don't judge or make fun of them. Kids can shower their pets with affection and count on a lick, a purr, a warm snuggle, or a feathery chirp in return. Caring for a pet helps children develop empathy, compassion, and an understanding that their actions matter.

Take time this week to recall the pets of your youth. Write about them in your journal, describe them to your children. Join in your children's natural connection with animals and absorb all the unconditional love awaiting you.

Don't feel guilty if you don't have pets. Many families aren't set up to care for one more living being. There are many ways to bring animals into your child's life. To follow are some ideas:

B A L A N C I N G   T I P S

Is there a neighborhood cat or dog your kids might become friends with? This eight-year-old girl told me about her important relationships with borrowed dogs: "Ozzie belonged next door but he spent most of his free time with me. He waited for my bus and wagged his whole body when I got off and ran to him. His teenagers didn't love him like I did. Ozzie died a while ago, and I was so sad not to have him around. No more Ozzie to steal burgers off our grill, to hug when I needed a friend, or to play with. But you know what happened? Another family moved into our neighborhood, and they are at work all day long. I get to go to their backyard and play with Kassie, their shaggy dog, and they pay me a dollar for my time. My mom says she should pay them. I guess Kassie has a little of Ozzie in her heart."

—⟩ Put up a bird feeder and notice which birds come. Try to recognize different bird sounds and imagine their meanings. A mother of
two was allergic to pet fur, but she included living creatures in her
children's lives: "I bought one of those see-through birdhouses and
attached it to the outside of the kitchen window. It comes with a privacy panel that you attach to the inside of the window that can be easily removed allowing the kids to take a peek. We have a mother bird
building a nest now, and the children are thrilled. They check on her
progress each morning when they come down for breakfast and even
include her in their prayers."

—⟩ Anytime a cat or dog we know passes away, we send the owners
a copy of Cynthia Rylant's touching children's book *Cat Heaven* or *Dog
Heaven*. Find books about pets that speak to your child's heart.

—⟩ My daughter isn't old enough to volunteer at our local animal
shelter, but she often collects old towels from friends to drop off for
the cages. A thirteen-year-old friend of ours volunteered this summer
to help out at a veterinarian's office. Her compassion for helping animals was put to good use. Could your child take action in some way to
advocate for unloved pets?

—⟩ I once heard someone say, "I wish I could be the kind of person
my dog thinks I am." We can. Talk with your kids about how easily pets
forgive, give love, ask for little, appreciate treats, jump through hoops,
and kiss away tears.

SCHEDULE A CHECK-UP

Just as you periodically replace the batteries in your smoke detectors, clean out your freezer, and put oil in your car, make an appointment this week for a parenting checkup.

Your appointment may be kept while you are commuting to work or writing in your evening journal. It doesn't much matter *where* you are as long as you are quiet and able to focus on yourself.

During this designated parent time, ask yourself the following questions:

- Am I present to enjoy the days I create?
- Will I be able to look back and say that I loved being a parent?
- When my kids are grown, will I have the joy of knowing that I was a part of the wonder and excitement of their childhoods?

Take the time to reflect on these questions and pay attention to how your mind wanders to them over the course of the week. What thoughts come up?

Joyce, a high-powered bank executive, made life-changing decisions after answering these questions. She says, "I hired a nanny to watch my kids, a housekeeper to do the laundry and cook, a lawn service to tend to my beloved flower beds, and someone to take care of the barn and the horses I had dreamed of owning. I drove seventy-five minutes to and from my job. Finally, I realized I was paying other people to live my life for me. These questions were the first step in examining my life, then I began to lay out a plan to change things."

Take a look at the pace of your typical week. Make a straight "laundry list" of the things you do each day. Check the list and see if there are tasks you might:

- Simplify
- Eliminate
- Delegate

By simplifying, eliminating, or delegating time-zapping tasks, we have more time to do what we love and more energy for the important aspects of our lives. Delegating doesn't mean you have to hire someone to take over a task. Of course, hiring a cleaning service, lawn help, child care, a professional organizer, or personal chef can be the answer to much of life's drudgery, but there are other ways to delegate.

An electric slow cooker (we used to call them Crock-Pots) was the answer to the evening meal crisis in my household. Around 5:00 P.M. each day, it would hit me that I had better do something about dinner. That was also the time my kids needed homework help, a hug or two, and a debriefing of the day. There was no option of eliminating the task of creating dinner and no one around to delegate to, so I simplified by throwing lots of fresh ingredients into the slow cooker first thing in the morning. By dinner, with a warm meal waiting, I felt as if someone had cooked for me.

Lisa is home full-time with two young children. She found that by simplifying her expectations, she is enjoying a more balanced life. "I gave up the idea of having a clean house all of the time. It distorted who I was as well as my time with the kids. So I do one thing a day, vacuum on Monday, laundry on Wednesday, and by the end of the week it all gets done."

Karen (a single mom) works long hours. After she spent some time considering what she might simplify, eliminate, or delegate, she decided to sell her home to move into a smaller house closer to her four-year-old son's father. She now spends less time commuting each week for Daddy visits and has a lot less house to keep up.

Have faith that there is a way for you to create more balance in your life. Try not to put barriers in front of the possibilities and solutions that come to mind when you answer the above questions. Remain flexible and aware that what works this week may be slightly off next week, but that doesn't mean you should give up.

Margaret, mother of three, realized that her barriers were the visions she held of what she should get done. She says, "Staying balanced is very challenging with all the demands from work, family, and life in general. I have finally found that in order to keep in balance, some things get done less frequently, or not at all, so I can spend time doing what I *want* to do instead of what I think I *should* do. So what if the boxes are still in the living room from painting the house four months ago or that the new puppy's toys are all over the house and backyard. Our time together as a family is brief because we all have so much going on. It is important to us to schedule time to have a family meal together—even if that means going out to a restaurant. Who says I *should* be able to whip up a restaurant-quality meal?

> *I weigh each decision and ask if it is beneficial to my life or the life of my son.*
>
> —KAROL, MOTHER OF ONE

> *Do what you can with what you have right where you are.*
>
> —THEODORE ROOSEVELT

THAT EMPTY FEELING

When we are unhappy, we often have an empty feeling we long to fill. We sense we're not getting what we want, so we set out to fill the void from the outside—a few chocolate chip cookies, a new pair of shoes, a glass of wine, a bit of gossip.

What does your child do when an empty feeling presents its ugly gap—whine, cry, cling, stuff another doughnut in a wide open mouth? Does he come down with a case of the gimmees, lash out with angry words, or tease his brother?

When we begin to accept that nothing from the outside world will ever be enough to assuage that empty feeling, we've crossed a huge chasm. With that empowering awareness, we can guide our kids to trust that they have unlimited wisdom within and realize everything they need is already theirs. This deep connection with spirit guides us and delivers only good.

So the next time you're feeling blue, instead of reaching for another piece of pie, place your hands on your heart, pause, breathe deeply, and imagine golden light filling your very being. Ask yourself, "What is the essence of what I am hungering for?" Then listen to the thoughts that surface. Maybe what you want more of is appreciation or security. How might you go about achieving these qualities? Just naming them often takes the edge off the longing.

The next time your child starts to whine, and you sense she's feeling an empty spot, try not to respond to the behavior but rather assume she is really craving more love. Remind her to turn up the spark of light that flickers inside. "Pretend you have a little switch right on your heart. Flip the switch on right now and feel that beautiful, powerful love filling you up."

Become an "empty feelings sleuth" and remain on the lookout for ways in which you and your child attempt to fill the void. Try saying, "I realize the Divine, rich source of happiness is within me." Remember Dorothy from *The Wizard of Oz* who discovered she needn't have gone looking outside herself to get "home"—the power was within her all the time.

―C

B A L A N C I N G   T I P

―C Spend some time this week journaling about your longings. Write about all that you crave. Detail what you want in life. Describe with words, and even with cutout pictures, your ideal home, car, body, job. Then take a look at what you've described. What is the essence of what you want? Is there a theme? Do you desire more beauty in your life? How might you go about creating that beauty now?

> *Spiritual force is stronger than material force; thoughts rule the world.*
>
> —RALPH WALDO EMERSON

SPIRIT ON WHEELS

I don't know about you, but often the only time I have my children as a captive audience is when we're all in the car. So I try to take advantage of that driving time as connection time.

When you hop in the car in the morning, turn off the radio or listen to serene music. If the kids protest, tell them they can tune into their music on the way home. Use this quiet time as an opportunity to listen to your kids. Ask them to describe how they'd like their upcoming school day to turn out. Ask if signs along the road can be signs for living. Stop. Yield. Caution. Then listen. You will be amazed at what this simple time might hold. Who knows? Maybe you have a backseat Emerson or Thoreau, whose words will be wise nuggets of truth.

Once drop-off is complete, you can turn the car into a spiritual oasis for yourself. This may be your only quiet time all day, so leave phone calls for the office. Say a prayer. Take a deep breath. Keep an uplifting book tucked in the door pocket for the inevitable waiting or traffic jams. *Living with Joy,* by Sanaya Roman, has been my car inspiration for the last few weeks.

BALANCING TIPS

—◦ When you hear the annoying "ding, ding, ding" of keys in the ignition, use it as a reminder to ignite your all-knowing, intuitive guidance.

—◦ Tape affirming words to your dashboard to remind you to: STAY CENTERED, BREATHE DEEPLY, REMAIN AUTHENTIC, LIGHTEN UP. Tape some affirming words to the back of the front seat for little ones to read: KIND WORDS ONLY, DON'T JUDGE, WORDS NOT WHINING.

—◦ Experience calm when you clear the clutter from your vehicle. Ditch the old newspapers, empty juice boxes, dried up Cheerios, and various toy pieces. Wipe the dashboard, mats, and steering wheel with lavender or rosemary oil–scented water. Stock the glove compartment with emergency baby wipes, granola bars, a bottle of water, and a few extra bucks—just in case. I leave some great-smelling citrus salve on the floor next to the driver's seat. When I hop in the car I put some on my hands, lips, elbows, and any child's hands, lips, and elbows within reach.

—☞ Maybe driving is your daily reminder to surrender and leave the driving of your life to God. Whew! Your car will take on a whole new meaning. You may actually look forward to your morning commute in your spirituality tank on wheels.

WHAT YOU SAY IS WHAT YOU GET

We have access to such a simple yet powerful tool to change the way we and our children experience our lives: our words. We can create a deeper sense of balance and harmony throughout our busy days by being conscious of our speech. Think of the old adage, "Be careful what you wish for; it just might come true," reworked as, "Be careful what you *say* for it *will* come true." If you want a frenetic pace, keep talking about how frantic you are. If, instead, you want a dose of serenity and calm, speak of yourself as being peaceful and getting things done with ease. Remember, you write the script throughout every moment of your spiritual voyage. To create happier events in your life, think and speak positively. Kick the negative talk habit and remind your kids to do the same.

An eleven-year-old girl gave me the best reason to try and use positive words with my children: "My mom always tells me how happy she is I was born and not just on my birthday. She says that these have been the eleven happiest years of her life. That makes me feel totally great, especially when she says it at the end of a tough day when school has gotten me down. It's nice to go to sleep feeling that someone loves me."

My friend Brenna, an actress, author, and mother of two says, "I've realized that my words are my magic wand that I weave throughout my day both in my dialogue with myself and others."

BALANCING TIPS

—☙ Pause before you speak, and clarify what you intend to say. Our words today can become our child's script later in life. Buddha's principal of right speech goes like this: "When we open our mouths to speak, let only the words that are loving pass through—heaven will be waiting on the other side."

—☙ The written word has tremendous impact. Leave uplifting words in your child's lunch box, under her pillow, in his shoe, written in shaving cream on the bathroom mirror.

—☙ Swearing is a bad habit that only demonstrates our limited word imagination. Let off steam by inventing a word that feels great to spit out, such as "Waldowanna" or "Cowabunga." Talk to your kids about the negative energy swearing elicits. If they swear, ask them if they know exactly what they are saying. Often, just describing the word's meaning embarrasses them enough to stop.

—☙ Gossip immediately brings down our energy, not to mention the person we are speaking about. If you want a big dose of negativity to upset your life, just start judging and criticizing others. Gossip is an energy boomerang—put it out and watch the discord rocket back into your day. You can't find the car keys, the post office clerk gives you a hard time about the way you've sealed your package, you stub your toe on the file cabinet, there's no ink in the printer, waves of nausea hit you on the way to the airport. You get the picture. Make it a habit to avoid rumors and gossip and your kids will do the same. Children absorb everything we say and mirror our actions. Give your child a model of a parent who speaks kindly about others.

—☙ Teasing words can zap a child's self-esteem and dampen his spirit. Make your home safe from put-downs and damaging words. One mom made a list of words that were off-limits, such as stupid, idiot, and hate. She charges her kids a quarter each time an offending word slips out.

—☙ Try to avoid comparisons and negative labeling. When you describe your child as "the naughty one" or "the one who never listens," she tends to live up to that description.

—☙ Ralph Waldo Emerson wrote that we don't trust our own words, but instead we choose to quote some saint or sage. Using descriptive words, describe your ideal balanced life. Write it down so you can quote yourself. For example, "I am living a flowing life that includes time for myself, my partner, and my children." (Describe just what you would do with that time.) "My career allows me to express my creativity and provides abundance for my family." (Describe the outlets you use to express and how you envision abundance.) "Spirituality weaves throughout my days and informs my every choice." (How does that spirituality look and feel?)

—☙ What are the first words out of your mouth when you see your child in the morning or at the end of the day? Kathy, mother of two, says, "I have always awakened my oldest child, now five, by saying

'Good morning, sunshine.' Now, with no prompting from me, she wakes up her little sister with those words in the morning. It's our morning wake-up call."

—☙ A mantra is a secret word or part of a sacred text that can lift us up no matter our age. Select a mantra for this week—"balance," "ease," "abundance"—something you would like to experience more of. Tuck it away in your mind and take it out when you have a lull in your day to fill you with the experience of what the word means. Help your child select a mantra such as "harmony," "peace," "joy!"

Words have the power to destroy or heal. When words are both true and kind they can change the world.

—JACK KORNFIELD

We are born with the power of the universe on the tip of our tongues.

—ANONYMOUS

Remember this: any word you speak with meaning will have power.

—ERNEST HOLMES

3

MARCH

SEVEN CORE CONCEPTS FOR
CONNECTED FAMILIES

You are linked with your children for a reason. You have somehow committed to spending your time on this earth together. Each day provides an opportunity to nurture the souls of those you love. It is possible. Your kids are never too young or too sophisticated to begin embracing the core concepts. No matter what your family might look like—and the *Los Angeles Times* recently came out with a survey that categorized over twenty-eight different types of moms in America today—you can begin now forging a deeper connection.

Yes, we are busy, but by choosing to embrace the seven core concepts, our lives will become more balanced.

Seven Core Concepts:

• **Tolerance:** Let the little things go. You won't remember the weeds in the front yard ten years from now, but you might recall your nine-year-old daughter's laughter as you taught her to throw a Frisbee— and *she* will too. Tolerance is also understanding that those we love might have different pictures in their minds of how events should play out.

• **Time Together:** This is what it's all about. Get creative and harvest more of it for your family. Plan special time, grab an occasional moment, turn routine events into family participation, share your hobbies, take part in your children's interests.

• **Trial and Error:** Never give up, continue to try new approaches for a deeper connection with your kids and your partner. Adjust to your child's changing age and interests.

• **Take It Out into the World:** Practice compassion in action as a family.

• **Teach Less, Listen More:** Honor each other's viewpoints and dreams—learn from your kids.

• **Tools for Living:** Begin creating your family's unique toolbox of beliefs. Be specific about what beliefs and values make it into that box, why they are there and how your family can put them to use.

• **Total Love:** You can't go wrong when you love deeply. Never assume that your family knows how much you love them—show them often.

DIRTY SNOW

Spring is trying to toss away winter's icy grip. Snow has been reduced to dirty clumps on the shady side of the street. I sit in my car in the eternal pickup line awaiting my daughter's school release. My attention is captured by a little girl dressed in a deep purple sweat suit—the sacred color used in Christian Lenten ceremonies, although I'm sure the Gap didn't have that in mind when they manufactured this outfit. She's doing a wild circle dance with her chunky snow boots leading the way. She swings and sways, throwing her purple-clad body into the frenzied dance. The exuberant child waves her arms and gallops freely. She's in stark contrast to the line of minivans and SUVs with bored-looking drivers sealed away from winter's last whispers. She tosses her black curls and flings her little body into the dance, beckoning her slightly older sister out of a waiting car to join her. Purple child meets green child and together now they prance in the muddy circle next to the exhaust-spewing vehicles holding exhausted parents.

I feel certain these dancing sprites are coaxing spring to us. In fact, I'm at the head of the line now and the brown snow clumps seem to have vanished and a few of the vans have opened their windows.

B A L A N C I N G   T I P S

⟶ Allow any child placed on your path to infuse you with her buoyant energy and spirit. Enter into her joyful approach to life, and yours will be invigorated.

⟶ Open your eyes to the wonder and delight of the changing seasons. The swing from winter to spring calls us to lift up and out of our self-imposed limitations. Choose to change and unfold into the person, parent, partner you wish to be.

⟶ Open the car window while you wait, breathe in the crisp air, smile at the stranger who passes by. As you open your heart to others, the busy chatter of your dictator mind will slow down. Your shoulders will drop. You will enter the present moment—a grand place to be.

MORNING SHOWER

About the only time I have completely to myself these days is my morning shower. In a way this morning necessity has become a spiritual ritual. I breathe deeply and allow the warm water to wash away any remaining sleepiness or worry. I imagine the pelting water is traveling deep into my soul and filling me with light and energy I'll call on throughout the day. I allow my mind to soften and remain open to the ideas that finally have a chance to be heard. Of course, this can't be a long meditative ordeal, as the morning routine in my busy household is just gurgling beneath the surface—not to mention running out of hot water. Usually someone bursts in looking for something—most often that something is me.

I recently heard former Massachusetts governor William Weld say that he wrote his first book, *Mackerel by Moonlight,* bit by bit after his morning shower. He would dash from the bathroom to a notebook on top of his bureau and, still wrapped in a towel, jot down ideas that had come to him while showering.

I suppose some might assume this morning meditation is a great multitasking technique. For me, however, the shower is just a home-made relaxation tank within earshot of any household emergency. It's become another habit of reverence, which doesn't require much time, effort, or special skill. I step into my day energized both spiritually and physically. I smell pretty good, too. Oh, and stay tuned for my next book—*Mimi by Morning Light.*

B A L A N C I N G   T I P S

— Make the bathroom a sanctuary from your busy household. Fill it with luscious magazines, wonderful scented oils stored in interesting glass containers found at thrift stores or yard sales, a basket of thick, white washcloths, candles, natural sponges, and fluffy white towels.

Make sure your kids each have a special towel and their own basket of goodies.

—☙ Design a sign to hang on the bathroom doorknob that reads: PARENT PONDERING! EMERGENCY ENTRY ONLY!

—☙ Keep a notebook or a pad of paper in the bathroom, call it "Shower Thoughts," and jot down all the inspiration and "to do's" that reveal themselves while your body relaxes under the warm water. (Can't someone invent a waterproof pad to attach to the shower tiles?)

—☙ Find other sanctuaries for yourself—the car, a hammock in the corner of the yard, a spare room. I have been threatening to turn my daughter's little wooden playhouse into my own cozy, thinking hut. A mother of three couldn't seem to find a sanctuary for herself; even the shower idea didn't fly. I suggested she explore the neighborhood around her office to find a quiet spot where she might escape at lunch. She discovered a tiny chapel, votive candles ablaze, that has become her welcome noontime retreat.

PARENT CHANTS

Studies have quantified the power of prayer to heal us. Experts have touted prayer as a tool for inner peace, tranquility, and acceptance. I can assure you that prayer restores my balance, nurtures my spirit, and eases my rambling mind.

Rather than thinking of prayer as petitions to a wish-granting God, imagine time spent praying, affirming, or meditating as shifting you to an open, expansive, loving well of power. Prayer nurtures you as you nurture those you love.

There are many types of prayer, and I encourage you to explore and discover what inspires you.

The following collection of words can be used as chants, mantras, prayers, or affirmations. There are some for mornings, when centering can be the launching pad for the day, and then those for day's end, when I've often felt like falling to my knees. However you use them, know there is power in turning within to the Source that guides you.

MORNING

I am open today to more
courage
patience
love

I don't allow the gloomy weather or the frightening news to intrude on my mood. With God I know I can do great things regardless of outer conditions. I am a positive force in the world and touch all those in my life with light.

I can be both a wonderful parent and fulfill my dreams. As I go out into the world I return to my nest revitalized. I am enough for my child.

God, help me to be a happy voice in my daughter's life today. It's a privilege to have this time with her. I don't want to hurry my way through these precious years; I want to savor every minute and have fun with our child. Help me take this responsibility seriously, but not too seriously. Help me to remember to laugh more. And give me the strength I need to be patient when I feel I have no patience left, to listen when my ears are full, and to forgive myself when I blow it. Her very life is a miracle to be treasured and respected. Thanks for giving me the opportunity to help this child grow.

—MOTHER OF ONE

Dear Spirit,
Please help me to remember
Who I am and to see my "real job" today.
Help me to live my life for the highest good
By loving myself unconditionally
As you love me.
And when I truly heal and love myself
Then, and only then, am I able to love another.
Help me to see the "light" in others
When they have forgotten it themselves.
And to help them, as guided,
To empower themselves.
I humbly give thanks for your help
In all aspects of my life.
And I know that everything is in Divine Order.
And so it is.
Amen

—STEPMOTHER OF THREE

With beauty before me, may I walk,
With beauty behind me, may I walk,
With beauty above me, may I walk,
With beauty below me, may I walk,
With beauty all around me, may I walk,
Wandering on a trail of beauty, lively, may I walk.

—NAVAJO PRAYER

Waking up this morning, I smile.
Twenty-four brand new hours are before me.
I vow to live fully in each moment
and to look at all beings with eyes of compassion.

—THICH NHAT HANH

END OF THE DAY
Homework hasn't been started
There's no dinner in sight
The dog needs to be fed and I'm so tired
Children are fussing, phone is ringing, we all need a hug
As I catch my breath and turn to you, Almighty Spirit, I know that all
*   is well*
Despite the chaos all around, you provide me with the ease to go on
Infuse me with your light and restore my center
Help me to be patient and loving and when I can't, to give myself a "time
*   out" until love returns*
Fill me with a fresh gust of grace to move through the rest of this day
Help me reach out to my family and share your light
Work through me so I might be You in action
Ah, Yes

Dearest Father / Mother / God,
May your healing light fill my child
May your loving energy soothe her pain
Bless her and renew her body as she sleeps
Amen

Almighty Spirit / All That Is,
Fill our home with order

Rebalance our equilibrium
Fill us with kindness
We are jumbled and confused
Align us with your peace

WHAT'S FOR DINNER?

My daughter Elizabeth, nine, just asked if her pal Emily can stay for dinner tonight. "Sure, but we don't have a special meal planned. In fact, we'll probably have scrambled eggs because I haven't even thought about dinner," I responded. Their faces lit up as they eagerly skipped off to continue their games, flush with excitement over being together well into the celebration of mealtime. The girls helped me to realize it's not so much what we eat that matters, but the people and attitudes we eat with that give mealtime significance.

Ask almost any adult about their childhood meal memories and you'll hear stories about the clean plate club, fights at the dinner table, power struggles, or guilt issues around food. They might also describe joyful family gatherings with laughter and connection, as soulful meals and memories were created.

Take a moment to look at your current family's relationship with food. Do you find yourself criticizing posture, manners, or inadequate vegetable intake? Are sweets used as a reward? Do kids have a say in the menu? Your mealtime mood, joyful and celebratory or dark and critical, shapes your children's lifelong liaison with food.

Even if it's pizza and carrot sticks tonight, notice your attitude and approach to eating.

BALANCING TIPS

—๏ Make cooking a celebration as well as connection time. When my kids were younger, I would get together once a week with a neighbor who was interested in healthy cooking. Her three children and my two girls were thrilled to play together while we cooked great batches of vegetarian chili, corn muffins, and lots of other goodies. We'd take our portions home and freeze them for the upcoming week. It was fun for the adults, saved time in the long run, and the kids had a blast. Since this neighbor has moved away, I now food swap with a friend occasionally. Anytime I cook a big batch of something, I make a little extra and drop it off at her house. She does the same. My kids love the magic of finding dinner on the front steps, and her daughter happily eats my soup when she won't touch her mom's.

—๏ Eating consciously is an awareness most of us have completely abandoned, if we ever experienced it in the first place. Try the following exercise with your kids. Take a raisin, or if they don't like raisins an apple slice will do, and sit quietly with your eyes closed. Take slow tiny bites and really taste the fruit. Describe the taste, the texture. Fully and completely eat that little morsel. Now, talk about how it may have tasted different from the handful of raisins you ate this morning in your cereal. Your mind was elsewhere this morning; now you are fully at one with the food.

There would be no more overeating if we all became more awake eaters. Next time you find your hand rhythmically returning to the potato chip bag, pause and begin to taste each chip. Call a quick "taste time" when kids are stuffing popcorn in their mouths while doing five other things. Everyone stops for a moment and really tastes their snack, accesses their hunger, and appreciates their food.

—☙ How do you cook your family meals—with an open, loving heart or crankily scrambling yet another egg for breakfast? The energy you put into preparing food is absorbed into your children's bodies just as surely as the protein or beta carotene.

—☙ Pause and bless the food you are about to eat. Think of beaming pure loving light onto the meal you are receiving. This action alone can enhance the energy of food. Ask your child to write a mealtime prayer as did this nine year old:

> *For my brain that helps me think*
> *For my teeth that help me eat*
> *For the grace that keeps me safe*
> *I give thanks.*
> *Amen*

Or try blessings from various cultures such as this Zen meal chant:

> *This meal is the labor of countless beings: Let us remember their toil.*

—☙ Add more candles and less criticism to mealtime. Increase conversation and decrease chaos. Temper the control and turn up the cheer.

—☙ Invite your kids into meal preparation and selection. When they peel the carrots, they are more likely to eat the carrots.

—ᴄᷝ The following quote from Jack Kornfield's book *After the Ecstasy* is posted on our refrigerator: "Strawberries are too delicate to be picked by machine . . . Every strawberry you have ever eaten—every piece of fruit—has been picked by callused human hands. Every piece of toast with jelly represents someone's knees, someone's aching back and hips, someone with a bandana on her wrist to wipe away the sweat." It keeps us mindful of all the human energy and toil that went into providing us with food.

—ᴄᷝ Allow your children to eat what they crave, within reason, and to eat when they are hungry, also within reason. When we are in touch with the natural callings of our body, our eating will be healthier than if we ignore our hunger signals. Some of us need little snacks all day while others have no morning appetite. It's not always easy, but there are creative ways to honor your child's natural appetite. Send the slow morning girl off to the bus with an egg sandwich to nibble along the way. Whip up a nutritious shake in the blender using frozen bananas and yogurt for the boy who prefers drinking his breakfast. We call ours Monkey Milkshakes, and they've been a favorite in our house for years. When all else fails I know my kids are getting good stuff in this special treat. The goofy name has stuck, too.

RECIPE

MONKEY MILKSHAKE

8–10 ounces of soy or rice milk—use Plus which is enriched with
   extra calcium
1 T flax oil—kids can't taste it and it's full of essential fatty acids

1 frozen banana—when they get brown and mushy just peel them
   and throw in the freezer

1–2 T protein powder—the kid-friendly brands taste great

1 T yogurt—vanilla or decaffeinated coffee flavor if you want the
   mocha taste

1 T wheat germ

Add any other frozen fruit (unless it's a mocha shake, in which case
   freeze decaffeinated coffee in ice-cube trays and toss in a few
   Java cubes)

Throw everything in the blender then adjust as necessary—more soy
milk if it's too thick, more frozen bananas if too thin.

The monkey milkshake should be thick, rich, sweet, and full of mocha
or fruit delight. You and your kids will love it.

*My happiest childhood memories are of Sunday
dinners with my family. It was the only day my
mom cooked anything other than hot dogs or sandwiches. She would make a roast of some kind and
there was nothing like those potatoes soaked in the
juices. All of us kids waited with wide eyes for
those Sunday dinners, just knowing Mom was cooking something special for us.*

—GAYLE, MOTHER OF THREE

JOURNEY OF THE TEEN

How many times have you heard people say, "The teenage years are
sheer hell"? or, "Just wait until your child is a teen. It's awful." Pretty

soon we start to believe this misconception about a stage of life. We begin to believe that when our children are teens, it *will* be a difficult time. What if we shift our thinking? What if instead of believing, and therefore creating, a situation of doom, we rephrase the popular belief? Instead we can say, "My radiant teenager is full of light, hope, energy, joy, and I accept her for all she is. We have a beautiful relationship."

Think about all the qualities you love in your child; then tell him what they are. Make a list of the good times you have had together and what they meant to you. Each time you think of your teenager in a negative way, reformat the thought. Use affirmations such as, "I let go and let God guide my beloved child to her highest good. She is a perfect expression of God's light." This doesn't mean you give her the keys to the car and turn your back—but rather release the struggle of any unattractive behavior and embrace the essence of your teenager.

Try to visualize how you would like your daughter or son's life to look. Create the picture as clearly as you can. Really take some time and fill in all the details. How does it appear? You can even do this together. Take time some evening to gather all kinds of magazines on the kitchen table. There's nothing like an art project to turn even a sophisticated teenager into an excited kid. Find some scissors, glue, and poster board. Cut out pictures of how you each would like your life to look and create your own "image board." Divide the boards up into sections for different aspects of your life. She might hesitate at first, but most kids can't resist the fun of this project. Hang your completed boards in a place where you will see them each day. Don't forget to cut out words to describe yourselves—"dynamic," "happy," "peaceful."

It can be difficult, but try not to tell your teenager how he is feeling. "You're going through a rough stage. I did as a teen and it's a lot about hormones." No one knows exactly how anyone else is feeling, and teenagers certainly think they know their own emotions unequivocally.

Remember that you are each spiritual beings just having a human experience—and learning together as you go.

B A L A N C I N G   T I P S

—☙ Schedule one-on-one times with your teenager each week, even if he protests and even if you have to drop another commitment. Nothing is more important than communication between the two of you, now more than ever. Let down your guard and try to come from a deep, wise, loving place in your heart when you speak. Be honest when you explain your worries. Instead of judging, speak from an "I" perspective. "I believe that everyone has a connection with spirit, even if you do feel so alone at times, and it sometimes takes exploring various options to feel that link." Remember that your older children want to tell you what they're feeling—they just don't know how to in a way they think you'll understand. Making time to listen assures them you are trying to understand.

—☙ I've heard it said that children are "assigned" an additional angel during the toddler and teenage years. Turn to that angel for guidance and inspiration.

—☙ Buy a new cookbook full of healthy meals and ask your son or daughter to pick out a recipe to concoct together. Mincing and mashing, stirring and stewing can draw you closer. Maybe your child would like to invite a few friends to take part in a taste test. Don't forget to light some candles. Make your home a place kids like to be, a peaceful and accepting place where they are buoyed up for the world out there.

—⌣ While teens may be compassionate about animal rights, the su. fering of the poor, or our dwindling water supply, they live a daily life filled with common cruelty. They snub the eccentric member of the science lab team, say unkind things about the overweight substitute teacher, laugh at each other's mistakes, and give the finger to the slow driver in front of them. Let's help our young adults slow down and think about what effect their actions have on others. Hold them accountable for their unkindness rather than avoiding the topic. Our job as parents isn't to win a popularity vote but to help our children succeed in all areas of their lives. Delivering a kind adult into the world is noble work.

> *In one of the most unexpected results of this survey,*
> *teenagers cited religion as the second strongest*
> *influence in their lives.*
>
> —*USA TODAY* WEEKEND SURVEY, 2000

GIVE ME JUST A LITTLE MORE TIME

We don't need all the recent polls to tell us that what parents want most is more time. We try to manage our precious time, but more often than not we feel as if time is controlling us—making us frustrated, short-tempered, annoyed, anxious, and pressured.

The other day I observed a frazzled mom pick up her daughter from kindergarten. She grabbed the little girl's hand and spun toward her idling car, quickly dropping her hand when the child couldn't keep up. The little girl scrambled behind her mom, shouting out details of her day. Her mother wasn't looking back.

How often do we hurry ourselves and our children, without realizing the harsh consequences of the dashing? Sure we can be patient when

n offer a helping hand when we don't feel pressured,
deep communication when we aren't rushed.

izabeth was creating a collage for school that was
represent aspects of who she was. There in bold letters was the
word TIME. I was surprised that the issue of time had wrapped itself so
intimately into my young child's consciousness. I took a hard look at
how I treat being on time, lateness in others, the amount of time to
complete a task, bedtime, quiet time. Am I hypervigilant about time or
is it simply the world I live in?

I am making an effort to shift my attitude, to stop viewing time as
something to be managed, and am trying to make peace with it. I've
realized that time management is about managing myself, not time. I
surprised myself when I recently said to my kids, "It's not the end of the
world if we're late."

The following ideas are to help you get a grip on the time issues in
your busy life.

B A L A N C I N G   T I P S

Overestimate the time you need to complete a task. Leave for
appointments five minutes earlier than you think it will take; if you
have free time on the other end, read a book or visit with your child.
This makes for less stress in the long run, and when it becomes a habit,
helps you create a manageable and balanced day.

Children need to be given the freedom to fully investigate their
present moment: a toddler exploring the pots and pans cupboard, a
thirteen year old daydreaming while listening to music.

⟋ Television can be a wonderful resource but most often it's a big time waster. If you use it to zone out after a tough day at the office, try substituting that thirty minutes with one of the Balancing Tips in this book.

⟋ Do you find you are constantly procrastinating because there simply isn't enough time to attend to all that needs to be done? Me, too. When I look around my life and see the unfinished list, anxiety strikes. Procrastination itself seems to be a time thief. Worrying about the incomplete item, rewriting it on a list, circling it, feeling guilty about not doing it, often takes more time than just handling it. This week, attend to one item you have been putting off. You'll love the freedom it brings. I've finally finished some long overdue paperwork. It took about fifteen minutes but had nagged at me for over two months.

⟋ Reward yourself for finishing tasks. I pour myself a glass of sparkling water in a crystal glass with lemon or lime when I finish making dinner. My little treat to myself. So often the mundane tasks of parenting can feel never ending. Create clear endings and applaud yourself along the way.

⟋ Take care of your health so you don't lose a day blowing your nose. Drink lots of water, take vitamins, cut back on sugar, and eat more fruits and veggies.

⟋ Begin practicing the three-quarter rule. Rather than stressing when the empty gas tank light pops up on your dashboard, fill the tank when it's three-quarter's empty. Same goes for staples in the pantry, laundry, paying bills. No more dashing out at midnight for a gallon of milk, searching for something clean to wear to work, or fending off the overdue bill calls.

With three kids in the house, there are many activities and parties to keep track of, so each year I buy a wall calendar. It has no pictures; just nice, big spaces for each date! Each child has a different colored pen for recording upcoming activities and commitments. This way, I can tell at a glance who needs to be where on which day. This system keeps me up to date and on schedule with each child's activities!

— MOTHER OF THREE

CELEBRATE SPRING'S ARRIVAL

In our busy lives, most of us have little time to connect with the great outdoors. And yet, marking nature's predictable rhythm can be a touchstone for our families. During a recent talk I gave, a mother of three, who yearned for her kids to maintain their relationship with nature, approached me. She said: "When my kids were younger I always took them to the playground, on hikes in the woods, outside to play with the dog or to look for animal tracks in the snow. Now there is no time for them to be outdoors unless it's organized. I think they miss that lovely time in nature, I sure do."

Mark March 20, the first day of spring, on your calendar and celebrate the magical shift of seasons—even if you never step outside. Whitney, my twelve-year-old, put forty tiny braids in her sister's hair this year to celebrate spring's arrival. Her experience braiding horses' manes came in handy on her sister's thick head of hair. Elizabeth was thrilled in the morning when she took out the braids and was transformed into a wild-haired spring creature.

The following ideas don't take much time, but by honoring nature's cycles everyday life takes on a richer meaning. Who knows, you may create an annual first day of spring tradition for your family.

BALANCING TIPS

— On your way home from work, pick up some flowers or small flowering plants for each child's bedroom.

— Let tonight's meal be the first picnic of the season—even if you're dining on a blanket in the living room.

— Write a spring poem and tuck it under your child's pillow to find at bedtime.

— Create a list with your child of all the spring treats the earth delivers—robins' eggs, green grass, warmer air, blue skies, purple crocus . . .

— Throw open the windows and imagine that the breeze, even a cold one, is blowing out stale energy and old habits that you would like to release. This can be the day to spring-clean your psyche.

— Get out your favorite mail order catalogs and have each child select a new bathing suit, shorts, or an outrageous beach towel.

—⌒ Create a spring parade around the neighborhood. Give the kids markers and a piece of poster board to make a sign that says, SPRING HAS SPRUNG!

—⌒ Have breakfast for dinner tonight and scramble up some eggs, the universal symbol of rebirth.

—⌒ Create a collage of your family's dream garden using pictures you and your child cut out of magazines and catalogs.

—⌒ Write your own myth. What might Father Winter say to Sister Spring as she knocks upon his heavy wooden door? Does he want to leave just yet? How does Sister Spring make her way in?

—⌒ As the sun goes down, light lots of candles, turn up your favorite music, and dance together to celebrate the beginning of spring.

—⌒ Head over to the nearest playground after dinner regardless of your children's ages. Swing into the spring air even if there is snow on the ground.

> *If a child is to keep alive his inborn sense of won-*
> *der, he needs the companionship of at least one*
> *adult who can share it, rediscovering with him the*
> *joy, excitement and mystery of the world we live in.*
> —RACHEL CARSON

Resources

PART ONE: WINTER

Adult Books

Ames, Louise Bates. *Your Ten to Fourteen Year Old*. New York: Dell, 1988. A hands-on guide for understanding the needs of children at this age.

Bender, Sue. *Everyday Sacred: A Woman's Journey Home*. San Francisco: Harper, San Francisco, 1995. A lovely short read to declutter your mind.

Coyle, Rena. *Baby Let's Eat!* New York: Workman Publishing, 1987. I've cooked from this little book since my children were born and the blobs of food stains can attest to that. The Applesauce Pancakes are still a favorite. We freeze any leftovers and pop them in the toaster oven for an instant breakfast on a weekday morning.

Dominguez, Joe, and Vicki Robin. *Your Money or Your Life*. New York: Penguin, 1999. Many people have told me that this book has turned their financial lives around. It advocates accounting for what is spent and an intense savings plan.

Grabhorn, Lyn. *Excuse Me Your Life Is Waiting*. Charlottesville, VA: Hampton Roads, 2000. This is a great book for focusing on what you want out of life. Its consistent theme is to *feel* that which you would like to manifest.

Kurcinak, Mary Sheedy. *Kids, Parents and Power Struggles: Winning for a Lifetime*, New York: HarperCollins, 2000. Practical ways to interact with your teen.

Mary Bray. *The Shelter of Each Other: Rebuilding Our Families.* New York: Ballantine Books, 1999. Many of my newsletter subscribers have recommended this book for reevaluating their views on family.

Ponder, Catherine. *The Dynamic Laws of Prosperity.* Marina del Rey, CA: DeVorss & Company, 1987. An inspirational guide for creating a flow of abundance in your life.

Orman, Suze. *The 9 Steps to Financial Freedom.* New York: Crown, 1997. This book has practical ideas and real-life examples, as well as exercises, to tap into your inner guidance.

Roman, Sanaya, and Duane Packer. *Creating Money, Keys to Abundance.* Tiburon, CA: HJ Kramer Inc., 1988. One of my favorites! The title is misleading in that the ideas can create an abundance of everything good, not just money.

Warner, Penny. *Healthy Snacks for Kids.* Chicago: Nitty Gritty Productions, 1983. What I love the most about this creative book are the notes I've made in the margins. It's like a little scrapbook of my children's early years. Next to Peanut Butter Pudding, dashed off in pink marker, is "Delicious. Whitney loves at 3½, Elizabeth at 9 months." Then below the recipe, scrawled in purple marker and childish handwriting, "Whitney made all by herself at age 5!"

Wolf, Anthony E. *Get Out of My Life but First Could You Drive Me and Cheryl to the Mall?* New York: The Noonday Press, 1991. The title says it all.

Kids

Edwards, Julie. *The Last of the Really Great Whangdoodles.* New York: Harper Trophy. 1999. A fantastic book about faith and possibilities written by the actress Julie Andrews. One of my daughter's favorite books at age nine.

Older Kids

Carlson, Richard. *Don't Sweat the Small Stuff for Teens.* New York: Hyperion, 2000. A wonderful gift for the teen on your list.

Covey, Sean. *The Seven Habits of Highly Effective Teens.* New York: Simon & Schuster, 2000. The more nonfiction, inspirational, action-based books written for teens the better.

Straus, Celia. *Prayers on My Pillow: Inspiration for Girls on the Threshold of Change.* New York: Ballentine Books, 1991. I love these true-to-life thoughts written by a mother for her teenage daughter.

————. *More Prayers on My Pillow: Words of Comfort and Hope for Girls on the Journey to Self.* New York: Ballentine Books, 2000. More wonderful prayers written by a loving mom.

Vanzant, Iyanla. *Don't Give It Away.* New York: Fireside, 1999. Girls need to hear more messages as positive as those in this book.

Web Sites

www.spiritualparenting.com. I've created this spiritual retreat for parents on the Web.

www.upromise.com. An incredible program that deposits money in your child's tax-free 529 college savings fund based on a percentage of what you spend with designated companies.

www.quicken.com. Information to get up and running with Quicken software. A great tool for organizing your finances. I can balance a checkbook for the first time in years.

www.smartmoney.com. A wonderful resource for investment tips, tax information, and college savings ideas.

www.stretcher.com. The Dollar Stretcher is a varied site full of ideas for saving money.

www.paymybills.com. Many parents swear by this on-line bill-paying service. They praise the time-saving benefits.

www.southernfood.miningco.com/library/crock/blcpidx.htm. Hundreds of recipes for the Crock-Pot. The vegetarian dishes and soups are especially good.

www.vegetarian.about.com/library/crockpot/blrecipes.htm. More Crock-Pot recipes—all vegetarian.

www.lhj.com/kitchen. Sign up for wonderful, speedy meal ideas delivered each weekday to your mailbox.

Magazines

O, The Oprah Magazine. www.ccare.hearstmags.com. 212-649-3843. Real ideas to try. Many, many busy moms tell me they read this magazine cover to cover. I've given subscriptions to my good friends. Even my husband sings the praises of this magazine.

Mothering Magazine. www.mothering.com. Santa Fe, New Mexico. 1-800-984-8116. This magazine has supported organic, natural choices for mothers for a long, long time.

Daughters. www.daughters@americangirl.com. 8400 Fairway Place, Middleton, WI 53562, 1-800-849-8476. This is a wonderful newsletter. It comes out eight times a year, for parents of girls ages ten to sixteen.

Zillions Magazine. 1-800-926-7845. A bimonthly magazine that helps kids learn about money and value.

PART TWO

SPRING

Are you in the midst of a transition of some kind? You're not alone. Go into any group and ask those who are experiencing a change in their lives to raise their hands. I guarantee you that at least 60 percent of the room will have their hands in the air.

Choosing change, however, is different from experiencing change you feel has been forced upon you—a spouse leaving, a job ending, an ill child. Active change brings us into the possibilities we've dreamed of. Reacting to change thrust upon us becomes a more intricate balancing act.

In the following months you will be offered tools and ideas for handling all kinds of change. You will begin to grab the moment and make it count, no matter what the circumstances are whirling around you. The thoughts to come will help you create a soulful home to shelter and sustain those you love, say no when you want to say no, and get a grip on parental energy. Balancing Tips will help you create a more unified family and nurture friendships to strengthen the web of loving relationships in your life—a web that cocoons you with grace during this vibrant season of change.

4

APRIL

NURTURE FAMILY CREATIVITY

Often in our rush for end results, an "A" on a spelling test, winning the soccer match, a piano recital, we unintentionally disconnect kids from exploring their creativity. Children, and their parents, need space in their lives to play with creative impulses without emphasis on performance. Try some of the following ideas:

1. Provide an environment that encourages your children to explore and play without interruptions. Schedule open-ended free time on your calendar if need be.
2. Rather than purchasing plastic toys with limited use, buy wooden blocks, art materials, musical instruments, or funky dress-up clothes from thrift shops.
3. Accept unusual ideas from your child by letting go of judgments and staying open to his naive wisdom. Just for today, try out his crazy suggestions for how to better frost that cake.
4. Use creative problem solving when everyday dilemmas come up rather than your word as the final verdict. "You guys decide if it's pizza or pasta for dinner by the time the bubbles are all down the drain."
5. Start an ongoing family story. Write an opening line and leave

the paper in a central place for others to add to as they are inspired.

6. Emphasize process rather than product. Put on music, spread out lots of paper, and ask your child to paint the music. Encourage her to focus on the movement of the brush and the swirl of color—rather than the end result.

7. Did you give up sketching years ago with the excuse that you just didn't have the time? Haul out your charcoal pencils and grab a sketch pad. Make a simple picnic lunch and head out to a beautiful natural setting with your child. Draw what you see, snack on treats, and revel in being creative together.

8. Allow your kids to be in charge of setting the table. They choose the evening's centerpiece design. Anything goes!

9. Even the youngest child can compose music. Ask the music lover in your family to "make up" a song on the keyboard or piano. Maybe the child's brother or sister can write some words to go with the notes.

10. Turn your largest doorway into a proscenium arch. You now have a stage for your child's performances. Hang two sheets on a tension rod and you have instant "entrance" possibilities.

GRAB THE MOMENT

My kids have different vacation schedules, which is a mixed blessing. It's delightful to have one-on-one time with each child, but a disappointment not to have a gala family respite from school and work.

Elizabeth is in the midst of her two-week spring vacation. We rented the movie version of Thorton Wilder's play *Our Town* and one simple line spoken by Emily has shifted my approach to these vacation days. Emily, who has died in childbirth, wants to revisit just one day in her life. As she goes back in time to her sixteenth birthday, she observes her family's morning activity and pleads, "Look at me, Mama, as if you really saw me."

There was my wake-up call. How often I rush through my days not really seeing those I love. In fact, I was there watching the movie, but my mind was preoccupied with work. I was reminded of a comment made by a mother of two. "Yesterday was my daughter's thirteenth birthday. As we gathered in the living room first thing in the morning to watch Kaitlin open her presents, I found, to my horror, that I was looking over her shoulder watching the clock on the mantel thinking, 'Would you hurry this up, I've got to get going this morning.' I was smiling at her, pretending to be excited about each item she opened, when really, I was feeling more and more anxious about my list of obligations to be attended to."

It shouldn't take a catastrophe for us to go back and cherish just one ordinary day with our kids. Life doesn't come with guarantees. Live all you can today—with gusto—it's a mistake not to.

B A L A N C I N G   T I P S

⁓ Say no to people who waste your time.

⁓ Say no to sacrificing the present for the sake of the future. A vibrant young attorney and father of two was part of an Internet start-up. He was working crazy hours and missed virtually every milestone in his two young children's lives. He kept telling himself that his working hard and long now was worth it because in a year he could retire and spend lazy days with his family. That was over two years ago, and he doesn't show any signs of slowing down.

—⟳ Say yes to your child's request for just one more story or push on the swing.

—⟳ Make it a habit to pause and really see your kids. Each time you hug them good-bye as they go off to school, look into their eyes and silently honor their essence.

—⟳ Jane, mother of two, has a great habit we can try. She says, "Every day I try and carry at least one of my children's 'lines' in my head. If I'm stressing over something, I imagine my child's face clearly and hear him saying that 'line.' Today, I'm hearing Daniel say, 'Thank you, Mommy.' He says it in such an adorable way."

—⟳ Take control of your time. Set goals, then break them into doable daily bits. Weave family goals with career and personal objectives. When goals are clear, you can better control your time and consciously carve out space for being with those you love.

—⟳ When an intimate moment presents itself, grab it—when your toddler reaches up with those incredibly luscious arms for a hug, hold him and dance together to the silent music only the two of you can hear. Pretty soon those arms will thin out and so will the opportunities for deep hugging, crazy dancing, and sweet, silent, toddler music.

*The golden moments in the stream of life rush past
us and we see nothing but sand; the angels come to
visit us, and we only know them when they are
gone.*

—GEORGE ELIOT

*Guard well your spare moments. They are like uncut
diamonds. Discard them and their value will never
be known. Improve them and they will become the
brightest gems in a useful life.*

—RALPH WALDO EMERSON

CHANGE YOUR THOUGHTS

If there is disharmony in our family, we'd like to fix it by naming the problem or correcting the offender. Yet how many times have we heard, "You can't change anyone?" As parents, it seems our duty to mold and form the life of another human being—our child. When they are babies, our kids rely on us for their very existence. It's tough to let go as they grow older. We can't always control our children's actions or arrange situations to make everything okay, but oh how we try.

What we can do is deeply influence all members of our family by creating the desired atmosphere within ourselves. We can control and manage our minds—thought by thought. We can create more love, understanding, and harmony in our families when our thoughts are more loving, understanding, and harmonious.

When family life gets bumpy, rather than reaching out to change everyone else's behavior, align yourself with the transformational power of Spirit within. Take a breath, put your hands on your heart, close your eyes, and reach into the deep well that sources you. Shift your thinking from, "He had better shape up and out of that bad attitude," to, "I am calm, centered, and patient. I listen to what my intuition tells me and to what my child has to say. I change *my* attitude." We experience the truest sense of peace when we slow down and take a look at our own behavior first. Our peace ripples out and affects our entire family. Think of yourself as the compass for your family and keep that compass aligned with your calm inner guidance.

> *The world in which we live is the exact record of our thoughts.*
>
> —EMMA CURTIS HOPKINS

MOVING ON

My mother-in-law died at home after a six-month struggle with cancer. Her granddaughters, my two children, wept anguished tears at her funeral. They mourned the loss of their lifelong friend and advocate. They ached for the empty spot in the big bed where she died.

We talked a lot about death as it crept closer and also about their grandmother's spirit beyond her sweet-smelling, cozy little house in the country. Whitney, who is twelve, did more listening than talking, and Elizabeth, nine, was in the moment with her questions, tears, and fears. She often needed to be held as sleep approached, to talk about the changes she saw in her grandmother, and her worries about what was to come. Whitney, on the other hand, appeared strong but was tucking the pain away from her family—it was a private struggle. She kept a prayer about death next to her bed.

Just as each child is vastly different, so is each child's response to and involvement in death when it spins into their orbit. It's our obligation as parents to be mindful of our children's differences and to honor their comfort zones in all areas but most especially when answering questions about the transition death brings.

It's our own work that first needs to be done—isn't that always the case? What are our feelings about death, heaven, the soul's journey? Let's ask ourselves how we can remain grounded in our own beliefs, indeed, what are our beliefs and how do we merge those with our child's needs?

Ask yourself how you felt about death as a child. If you're like most of the adults I've worked with, you were afraid your own parents would die. Elizabeth pulled me into our dark living room one evening when her grandmother had taken a turn for the worse and, with tears rolling down her sweet cheeks, said, "I'm scared that you and Dad will die. I don't want anything in the house to change, I don't want you or Dad to take any trips. I just want things to stay the same. I'm afraid if anything changes, I might not remember Marty [her grandmother] anymore and all I have is my memory of her."

I'm grateful my kids were able to cry at their grandmother's funeral—crying releases the hurt. I cried right along with them. Grief doesn't disappear, but when we grieve as we go, we free our spirits from the great effort of holding the pain inside.

BALANCING TIPS

⎯◌ When your child asks a question about death, listen carefully before responding. If it isn't a good time to focus on your child, set up a time when you can be fully attentive. "I can't pay close attention to your very important question right now, but let's take a walk after dinner, just you and me, and talk about it."

—☙ Ask questions before answering your child's questions. What is it she wants to know? Her answers will help you gauge where the concern is and how much information to give.

—☙ Use the opening remark, "Some people believe . . ." when you want to give a global view of death.

—☙ Ask your child to write about his feelings, or if he is too young, to draw a picture. These intimate peeks at your child's view of death and life after death are illuminating.

—☙ Losing a pet can be traumatic for kids no matter their ages. I can remember vividly when each of my childhood pets died. Make sure to be sensitive to your child's grief—cut back on activities if that seems to be a balm, create a scrapbook of the pet's life if that feels helpful. When my friend Emily's dog died she created a memorial of sorts for him in the mudroom where he slept. On a bench, right next to the children's coatrack, was a photo of Max, his leash, his favorite fetching ball, a little vase of flowers, and good-bye cards made by each of her children.

—☙ Losing someone we love can knock us off balance for quite some time. But everyone has a different time frame for mourning. Respect your children's reactions to death as being different from yours and from each other's.

—☙ Be cautious about saying that God wanted the dece
heaven. This sets up some frightening issues for kids. "If (
my grandmother, then I had better be bad so God doesn't wa...
or, "I don't want to get close to a God who might take me from my
mom."

—☙ When you are in the midst of a crisis—a death, divorce, or seri-
ous illness—finding balance seems impossible. Go easy on yourself.
Don't judge your day or week by what you have accomplished—just
creating a loving home for your children and an occasional meal is an
exemplary job.

—☙ Ask your friends, family, and neighbors for help. Think of it this
way, it is so much easier to give than to receive and by asking for help
you are providing a great service to someone else. You are gifting them
with the opportunity to give.

—☙ Keep up the seemingly ordinary rituals built into your family
life—mealtime prayers, lighting a candle in the morning, waffles on
Saturdays, pizza for Friday night dinner. The order and predictability
can create just the structure your child's soul is longing for.

> *There are no bright colors or patterns in heaven.*
> *No reds only light pinks and yellows. There are no*
> *designer clothes there.*
>
> —AGE 8

> *To weep is to make less the depth of grief.*
> —SHAKESPEARE, *HENRY VI,*
> PART THREE, ACT II.

SOULFUL HOMES

Austrian philosopher Rudolf Steiner proposed that children's immediate physical home environment shaped their future emotions and approach to life.

Our homes are also visual representations of how we feel about ourselves—expressions of our inner lives. Home is our spiritual center, the first place from which we observe the world, our shelter from the intrusions of the outside. I'd like to invite you to ask yourself, "What is it within me and my family that can find expression in my home? What gives me a sense of harmony and how can I bring more of that into my living space?"

The urge to create sacred spaces is uniquely human. Whether we do it by having quiet time in the garden, a special chair in which to rock the baby while we pray, or a collection of memories on a corner table, all of us have a need for a physical reflection of our spiritual selves. Even in a busy household filled with the vibrant energy of a growing family, there are opportunities to weave sacredness through the tangle of dirty socks and pet hair. We can add nuggets of soulful decorating to create family spirit regardless of whether we rent or own, are color blind, or haven't time to set the table, much less iron linen shams.

It's wonderfully grounding to bring nature inside by adding plants or decorating with elements of nature, such as stones for cabinet pulls, starfish as mantel decorations, tree branches aglow with little white lights, discarded nests as centerpieces. Taking down the heavy curtains allows the light to pour in.

Family spirit flourishes when there are nooks for kids to read in, ways for clutter to be dealt with, safe cleaning supplies to use, scaled-down visuals so that simplicity or precious collections become the theme. When our home is a safe oasis, we can recharge there after being in the world outside—whether our world is high finance or second grade.

BALANCING TIPS

In my experience, about 30 percent of the "stuff" in children's rooms is no longer used—outgrown clothing, toys with missing pieces, books that are no longer of interest, artwork that could be stored. The effects of a cluttered room include: feeling out of control, a sense of heaviness, depression, a lingering chaotic energy, and even exhaustion. Set aside a special "create order" day with your child. Buy storage bins in fun colors, huge trash bags, and put on your favorite music. I find Aretha Franklin makes organization lots more fun. Throw open the windows, regardless of the temperature, and together begin to declutter and organize your child's possessions. When you're done, celebrate in a way that is meaningful for you and your child.

A friend of mine grew up in a family with nine children. Her strongest memories are not the chaotic noise of all those kids but the joyful sounds of music. Someone was always playing an instrument or a record was spinning on the hi-fi. What is the sound your child most often hears? Borrow CDs from the library and try different music. I'm a big advocate of soothing music in the mornings to move us into our day in a calm way.

Another friend tells of the "kisses box" that meant so much to her growing up. Her father traveled a great deal and would always pack this little heart-shaped box that the children had filled with their kisses.

There is an ancient law requiring Jews to affix mezuzahs, tiny boxes with Scripture passages rolled inside, to their doorways. Doors are our thresholds to and from the shelter of home. How might you mark yours to both welcome weary travelers back and launch enthusiastic voyagers onward? My daughter used to have a small erasable memo board attached to her bedroom door with designated lines for messages and a pen hung expectantly with a bold fluorescent cord. She eagerly awaited greetings on her, always open, door. Now that she is older, that board is no longer there, and that door is often closed. Her threshold marker now hangs on the inside of her bedroom door, a beautiful photograph of grazing horses. This equestrian vision is what she sees each day as she leaves the oasis of a butter yellow comforter and a warm, black-and-white kitty for the complicated halls of middle school.

—ᶜᵒ Parents are the gatekeepers of the home, and with that role, I believe, is the responsibility for what enters into our havens. The culture of the outside world has the power to penetrate our walls when we sign up for cable stations with disappointing programming, rent inappropriate movies, listen to lyrics that compromise our values, or buy toys that symbolize violence. I'm not naive enough to believe that reality doesn't seep into our soulful homes; of course it does. But reality becomes more manageable for our children when home is a forum for discussion, and together we decide what is worthwhile or disagreeable. When we talk about the distressing news we've heard on the radio, debate the merits of renting a particular movie, and discuss a book we've all read, we make our home more than just a lull from the world.

—ᶜᵒ I've often said that kitchen tables are the heart of the home and refrigerator doors the soul. When we gather at the table, no matter what it is we are eating, we each have our own place and we belong. Eating together, talking together, gazing into one another's eyes over candlelight links us forever. And oh how I dislike the new refrigerators that aren't magnetic. Where else might we hang beautiful artwork, splendid report cards, photographs of those we love, clippings for all to read as we go looking for cold milk and an apple?

—◌ My daughter had a recent school assignment that asked her to take a journey through the rooms in our home and write about five handmade items she found. It alerted us to the objects rich with meaning sprinkled around our house. Elizabeth wrote about the quilt hanging on the back of the white wicker rocking chair in her bedroom: "The quilt was made for me by my mom when she was pregnant. It has both light pink and blue patterns and colors because she wasn't sure if I was a boy or girl yet. This object is dear to me because it is the last sewing project she ever did." She's right about that—unless you count the button I reluctantly sewed on her khaki pants. She noted the colorful stair pads leading to our basement that her great-grandmother had made over sixty years ago and the funny old woman made out of clay, Mrs. Stein, that my mother gave me when I left home for school. Mrs. Stein, wrapped up in an old coat, scarf, and black boots has watched over me in every dorm room, apartment, and home since then.

Take your child's hand and wander through your home observing those handmade items that call to you to tell their story.

> *No matter under what circumstances you leave it,*
> *home does not cease to be home. No matter how you*
> *lived there, well or poorly.*
>
> —JOSEPH BRODSKY

SUPPORT CHILDREN'S INTUITION

One of the most important things we can do to create an ideal childhood for our kids is to keep their intuition intact. When we help our children trust and follow their intuition, we keep that inner child alive for the rest of their lives.

Webster's Dictionary defines *intuition* as "the immediate knowing or learning of something without the conscious use of reasoning; instantaneous apprehension." This is a fairly good definition, but intuition can be even more. Benjamin Hoff, the author of *The Tao of Pooh,* writes that "intuition is being sensitive to circumstance." A wise seven year old says, "It's when I just know inside what I should do."

As adults, we fret, worry, and calculate, but we often aren't in touch with what goes on around or within us. We break decisions down and look at all the pieces, forgetting to look at the whole. We analyze when the decision would often be easier if we just went with our gut.

J. Robert Oppenheimer, one of the pioneers of nuclear energy, once remarked, "There are children playing in the streets who could solve some of my top problems in physics because they have modes of sensory perception that I lost long ago." Perhaps we adults might take the advice of Yoda, the wise, childlike character in the *Star Wars Trilogy* films, who tells us, "You must unlearn what you have learned."

Intuition allows us to be more than just computers that calculate. In this technological age, it is important that our children have rich opportunities to put their hunches, gut feelings, and intuition to work. It will be their ever present guide as they move through life—reliable, consistent, and foolproof.

When my youngest daughter was two years old she surprised me with her intuitive ability. We sat in a circle of adults and older children with about ten household items placed in the center of the circle, measuring spoons, cheese graters, whisks, etc. Everyone closed their eyes while one of the items was removed. Upon opening our eyes, we were asked what was missing. Five out of five times this tiny child was the first and often the only one to know immediately what item had been removed. Had the older kids and adults lost their connection with their expanded awareness?

Our children operate naturally from their inner wisdom. When we enhance their willingness to trust this insight and combine it with logic, the entire family unit shifts into a more balanced state.

BALANCING TIPS

⁓ Acknowledge, respect, and act on your own intuition. Tune into it daily. Follow your hunches in all areas but especially in your role as a parent. What feels like the right decision to make? What does your gut keep telling you to do?

⁓ Be flexible, spontaneous, and willing to take action on your children's ideas and inspirations.

⁓ Pay attention to throwaway, or off-the-wall comments your kids make.

⁓ Be original when responding to each of your children. Don't feel you must have a "one size fits all" method of relating to them. Different kids respond to different styles of parenting.

⁓ Create an atmosphere in your home where it is safe to take risks.

—☍   We are a culture that is quick to categorize children from an early age. Be open and aware of your child's very individual way of approaching the world rather than limiting him by a label.

—☍   Find a school or day-care situation that respects and honors children's natural wisdom. Don't settle for less, there are always options. Follow your intuition and open your unlimited possibility thinking.

—☍   Practice letting go of total control in your family. Assume that your kids innately have a sense of what's right for them. Allow them to develop their own answers from what they think, feel, and know, then support them in this discovery. "What do you think is the best way to stop the headaches you've been getting?" "You are in charge of planning what we do on Saturday." Give your kids many opportunities to make choices. Their intuition grows stronger as a result, and the responsibility that goes along with their choices helps them grow.

—☍   Remember those *Where's Waldo?* books? Haul them out of the closet and play "Let's find Waldo with our inside eyes." Just breathe deeply and let your intuitive sense guide you to Waldo. Your kids will amaze you with their aptitude at this game of intuition. It's great practice.

—☍   When making a decision, shift from a purely intellectual approach and encourage your children to do the same.

> *I did not arrive at my understanding of the fundamental laws of the universe through my rational mind.*
>
> —ALBERT EINSTEIN

SPIRITUAL LATITUDE

My daughter is immersed in a project on longitude and latitude for her Math Fair at school. The opening line of her report reads: "Since the beginning of time, people have asked the question, 'Where am I?'"

Elizabeth has become a cartographer, creating the earth with a beach ball wrapped in papier-mâché. With the dot of a permanent marker she shows me where we exist—our chunk of earth, measured by her calculations, and some horizontal and vertical strands of orange yarn.

There isn't such a tidy system to answer the other age-old question we humans have asked, "Why am I?"

Archaeologists have unearthed thousands of paintings, sculptures, and engravings that reveal our earliest ancestor's attempts to sort out this question.

For centuries, religions have identified codes for living and consequences for lives lived wrongly to assuage our need for guidance with the "Why am I?" dilemma.

Science has organized our world so we can place ourselves on a geographic grid—comforting for my nine-year-old mathematician. But what of her questions about the purpose of her life on this complicated very real Earth?

When children are young, they naturally express their colorful personalities. The veil seems to drop down, however, around the age of nine or ten. That vibrant self becomes a bit muted, and the spiritual longing of "Why am I?" arises.

Let's help our children uncover the wishes of their hearts, find the latitude of their souls, and identify their higher purpose for living. Let's reignite our own dreams, passions, goals, and high intentions that we may have lost in the diapers and deposit slips.

BALANCING TIPS

—๛ Read C. S. Lewis's *The Chronicles of Narnia* as a family. If your children are twelve or older encourage them to read *The Four Agreements* by Miguel Ruiz.

—๛ Tell your kids the story of their birth and how you felt upon their arrival.

—๛ Help children recognize and accept the Divine Presence as the great reality running through their lives. Do so by pointing out examples of how this Presence works with and through us in our everyday ups and downs.

—๛ Share your own journey of uncovering the longings of your heart. Give kids a vocabulary for and validation of their soul's inevitable quest for a vital, important, acknowledged life. Don't assume their ego is playing for power. You might recall some adult's voice from your own childhood, "Who do you think you are?" "Miss Too Big for Her Britches." "Don't get a big head." Let's not shame our children as they play with their reason for being.

—๛ Support your child's dreams, wishes, and hopes. Think of them as spiritual promptings—within those dreams may lie their Divine potential. Sure, they'll change and vary, but note them as they arise. A passionate eight year old told me, "My dream is to live on a farm and have lots of animals. If I keep the picture of that farm in my mind, when I grow up it will happen."

⟶ Use an ink pad and make fingerprint marks with your young child. Point out that no two people have identical fingerprints. No two blades of grass are alike, nor are two leaves on a tree. We are created as unique individuals—filled with our own gifts.

I leave you with the words of author Julia Cameron: "We can trust the benevolent flow of the universe, that we are not flawed, that our dreams are not tainted, that we are intended to expand, and that God expands and expresses through us."

Enjoy your child's expansion as he or she seeks to discover, "Why am I?"

> *There is a real you, which lives in a real God, and the two are one.*
>
> —ERNEST HOLMES

5

MAY

FAMILY UNITY

Do you think of your family as a connected unit? Kids long for connection, and when they feel the pulse of belonging to something grounded and good—their families—they are able to go out into their worlds wrapped in that security. Sure there are ups and downs; but when we are united with others who care for us, the downs are less bitter.

Time and time again parents ask me for a way to check on their family unity. They wonder how they are doing, if their family is working well as a unit, and what they can do to create more cohesion.

Below is a simple checkup to help you get a read on where you are. Remember, your family is living a spiritual experiment and it is in the ebb and flow, the yin and yang, the ups and downs, the openness to change, that you grow closer to each other.

Set aside a few minutes to take the checkup, then jot down any ideas that occur to you when it's complete. Go easy on yourself. The point is to find everyday opportunities for connecting, not to feel inadequate or diminished about your current family situation.

Family Unity Checkup

Respond to the following questions with True or False:

T   F

☐ ☐   I have a scheduled, predictable time to gather with my family for fun.

☐ ☐   I have discussed family rules and consequences and evaluate the appropriateness of these rules every six months or so.

☐ ☐   I tuck my young child into bed each night I am home or spend time with older kids.

☐ ☐   We eat at least one meal together most days.

☐ ☐   "Put-downs" and mean-spirited teasing are not allowed in my home.

☐ ☐   We have laughed together at least once this week.

☐ ☐   We listen to each other with respect even when we disagree.

☐ ☐   I know what my child worries about.

☐ ☐   We talk about our family traditions, history, and ancestors.

☐ ☐   We have predictable opportunities for each family member
to be heard, family meetings, a family journal, open discus-
sions at mealtime, carpool conversations.

☐ ☐   I know my child's favorite song, music group, or sports team.

☐ ☐   Our family watches less than seven hours of television a
week.

☐ ☐   I don't expect perfection. Trying hard is applauded and lessons are learned from mistakes.

☐ ☐   Our family strives to live agreed upon spiritual beliefs and
we often discuss how to do so.

Tally up your True and False responses and take a look at your score.

1–2   False: You're doing amazingly well keeping your family
connected in a stressful world!

3–5   False: Your family could use some strengthening.

6+   False: Your family definitely needs to set aside more time
for one another.

Family Affirmation

We each contribute something different to this family.
We are a harmonious whole.
We are a cohesive team.
We move through any difficulty with grace.
We communicate.
We choose love rather than criticism.
We are guided by God's light.
We take this light into our world.

The Way is long—let us go together.
The Way is difficult—let us help each other.
The Way is joyful—let us share it.
The Way is ours alone—let us go in love
The Way grows before us—let us begin.

—ZEN INVOCATION

YA GOTTA HAVE FRIENDS

For my birthday last year, my husband arranged for my dearest, far-flung friends to surprise me in New York City for a girl's weekend. I was zapped with enough positive, nurturing, loving energy from these four women to last me another few years.

We don't need oodles of pals to have complete lives. Who has time? But one or two close, trusted friends can sustain the spirit like balm to a burn. Our kids learn about friendship from their teachers—their parents. If they see friendship as a laughter-filled, generous-spirited, genuine give-and-take, they'll approach their own relationships with that expectation and with those actions.

It takes a certain maturity for kids to forgive their friends along the way. It's not easy when your daughter isn't invited to the sleepover, or your son's idea is shot down. We can help them come up with strategies for coping with the hurts in order to sustain friendships that will ripen with time.

We might even add a few traditions to our kids' friendships. "Every year I have Elena over on Valentine's Day for a special tea party" or "Ted sleeps over every year on the night before my birthday—even if it's a school night." How about creating a mother-son book club or a father-daughter outing group? The members don't have to be pals, but by meeting consistently with a common theme, a soulful connection can be created.

In our busy lives, nurturing friendships is often the first thing to go, at least in my experience. In all the whirl, we don't seem to notice its absence until there's a little tug of loneliness. "Oh, it would be so nice to meet a good friend for dinner." Our children feel the same longing. Sure they see kids in school, at practice, on the bus. It's not the same, however, as just hanging out talking or weaving their vivid imaginations together through play.

Friendship is a sweet grace that can flow throughout our lives. Make your home "friend friendly" and nurture and support your child's growing friendships. Don't forget your own treasured friendships and carve out space in your week to reconnect in some way: E-mail, notes, phone calls, exercising together.

Maria, mother of a newborn, came up with a unique way to spend time with her friends: "I crave my female friends but don't have time to see them now that the baby is born, so I invite them to grocery shop with me, and we spill our secrets while squeezing pineapples."

BALANCING TIPS

⟶ Try not to judge your child's friends. Support him as he learns discernment.

⟶ Emerson said something like Be a friend to make a friend. His words were much more eloquent, but the idea is simple and understandable to the youngest of children—teach it to yours. We must become that which we desire.

—೬ Make your home an inviting spot for your kids to bring their friends. That doesn't mean you need the latest video games, just an accepting heart and lots of snacks.

—೬ Make sure your older children are connecting with friends in real time, not just instant messages via the computer.

—೬ Aristotle wrote: "Our feelings towards our friends reflect our feelings towards ourselves." Maybe you can mull that over with your family the next time you have a dinner discussion and someone is criticizing or applauding a friend.

—೬ Instigate a family policy that it's not okay to "drop" a friend or "dump" a date. As adolescents explore relationships, this is a common occurrence. It's hurtful and damaging, and you can take a stand against it.

Friendships begin because, even without words, we understand how someone feels.

—JOAN WALSH ANGLUND

And let there be no purpose in friendship save the deepening of the spirit.

—KAHLIL GIBRAN

CREATIVE FLOW

I've had the delightful opportunity of leading writing workshops with people of all ages. I find that simple writing exercises can provide many of us with vivid inspiration and enlightenment. Stream of consciousness writing—whether on a napkin while sipping our morning tea, in a child's cast-off coloring book while overseeing a sandbox play date, or in a fancy new journal on the train ride to work—can anchor us more deeply within ourselves while unleashing our creative energy to sail into all areas of our lives.

This kind of writing isn't necessarily pretty or fluid; it is simply about putting pen to paper and allowing ideas to flow. When we begin to open our creative channel, many gentle but powerful changes unfold. Creativity is our Creator moving through us. Our parenting selves, our working selves, our spiritual selves are richer as a result. According to a recent study released by the American Medical Association, even our physical selves are healthier when we write.

One of the writing prompts I often use with groups to warm up and get the words flowing is your "assignment" this week. This exercise might shed some interesting light on your own childhood.

Don't edit or worry about the outcome, just set aside twenty minutes and finish this thought:

Sundays in my house were_____

BALANCING TIP

⌁ Grab your journal before you go to sleep at night and jot down a few images of your child from the day. When you go back and read these simple, short entries years from now, your memory will be stimulated and deliver to you simple snapshots of your son or daughter. A few words can evoke powerful images. Capture the everyday moments of your family life in words, and chronicle your journey together.

—☙ Write about your current home as if you were an outsider looking in. Describe what you see, hear, smell, and sense.

—☙ Fill in the sentence that begins, "When I am busy I . . ." Now, write the ending to the thought, "When my life is in balance I . . ."

We must accept that this creative pulse within us is God's creative pulse itself.

—JOSEPH CHILTON PEARCE

All writing is dreaming.

—JORGE LUIS BORGES

I put a piece of paper under my pillow, and when I could not sleep I wrote in the dark.

—HENRY DAVID THOREAU

KINDNESS COUNTS

One of the most common questions parents ask me is," "How, in this materialistic, competitive world can I raise kind children?" My answer is to begin by being a kind adult. When your child sees you go the extra mile to help a friend, carry someone's groceries, make a meal for the new family that just moved in, or invite people into your life who aren't exactly like you, he will naturally see loving kindness as the way to live. We are mirrors for our kids, and when they observe our examples of kindness, they'll know where to begin.

One day I mentioned that I had a tummy ache. My nine year old dashed up the stairs to run a bath, turn down my bed, and lay out my favorite nightie. "You know who" had treated her tummy aches in just such a way.

Kindness is a quality that isn't often rewarded in our schools, so we must make a strong effort to acknowledge it at home. Kids are naturally empathetic from an early age: as newborns, they cry when they hear another baby crying; they offer their favorite doll to the friend who has scraped a knee. We tend to expect our young children to grow out of this compassion and become self-absorbed. "Oh it's the terrible twos," we say. "Kid's just can't share at this age." What if we shifted our expectations and saw our kids as truly caring beings? Boys in particular are often rewarded for being clever or assertive, but not often for showing compassion.

Chrissie, a mother of two, is making an effort to acknowledge her young son's kindness. She recalls, "I rode with the second grade on the bus to the zoo. Michael sat next to a classmate who uses a wheelchair and is mentally impaired. I was amazed at how helpful and considerate he was, and I was quick to tell him so when we got home."

Kindness, empathy, compassion, and love grow from appreciation and respect, and in turn create more of both. Instead of comparing kids and fostering competition—"You have the best voice in the choir"—it would be helpful to applaud their thoughtfulness. For example, you could say, "I liked the way you complimented Amy's painting."

Weave some of the following ideas into your days to encourage your child to show kindness:

B A L A N C I N G   T I P S

—⌒ Treat your child with respect. Never do something to a child that you wouldn't like done to you.

—⌒ Read books about compassionate heroes who have gone before us, such as *Buddha* by Demi and, for older children, *The Dalai Lama: A Biography of the Tibetan Spiritual and Political Leader* also by Demi.

—⌒ In an achievement-oriented culture, we may focus more on grades and sports victories than on values of the heart. Take the time to acknowledge kind actions as having true worth. Perhaps you might begin a Kindness Journal and each time a family member does something kind, he or she can jot it in the journal.

—⌒ Ask your kids to come up with a list of everyday opportunities to show kindness.

Some ideas to get started:

- Smile at the bus driver.
- Compliment at least one person a day.
- Hold the door for the person behind you when you come in from recess.
- Pass on to someone else a book that really touched you.
- Offer to walk a neighbor's dog.

- Write a letter to someone you read about, care about, would like to get to know better, or write a note of encouragement to someone who has just received sad news.
- Help someone find something they have lost.
- Recycle magazines to the local library.
- Help a younger sibling with homework.
- Sit with the kid who usually sits alone on the bus.
- If kids are speaking unkindly about someone, take a stand against it.
- Bake an extra batch of cookies and leave them on a neighbor's doorstep.
- Wrap up toys you no longer use in pretty tissue paper and pass them along to younger kids who might enjoy the surprise.
- Pick up around your school or neighborhood.
- Look in your friend's eyes and listen even when you really feel like talking.
- Hug somebody who needs it.

You cannot do a kindness too soon, for you never know how soon it will be too late.

—RALPH WALDO EMERSON

SAFETY FIRST

Children need to feel safe to explore their universe. When their physical and emotional needs are met, their spirits are free to flourish.

Even though it feels as if we are spending huge amounts of time tak-

ing care of the basic earthly needs of our families, with no energy left for
the soulful stuff, I want to ask you to give your home environment a
simple age-appropriate safety check this week.

Do you have fire extinguishers on every floor of the house? Does
your child know how to use one? Designate an annual date you change
the smoke detector batteries, such as the first day of school or a child's
birthday, so you never forget. If you have toddlers, plug in those little
plastic outlet covers. If you have a new driver, make sure he knows how
to change a tire and invest in a car phone for emergency use only. (You
can dial 911 on any cell phone, even those that are inactive.)

Make sure you have an escape plan in case of a fire, emergency
phone numbers available, a designated neighbor to whom children can
go in case of an emergency. Show kids how to put out a stove fire, call
for help, tend to a cut, lock the doors.

Scan your child's support system. Does he feel secure with his camp
counselors, teachers, or day-care providers? What about her siblings?
Does your child have friends to turn to or another adult in her life to
confide in if she needs additional support?

Regardless of your child's age, take some time this week to think
about safety; then take some action to change things if they need adjust-
ment.

MOTHERING IN THE LIGHT

I always look forward to Monday afternoons as this is the time Elizabeth
has her piano lesson. This week was no different. I brought my journal
and some letters that needed a response and settled in outside as the
sounds of piano music wafted out the open window.

Lyle, the little boy who has a lesson before Elizabeth, bounded by me to his awaiting mother and toddler brother. I noticed a flurry of activity around Lyle's car and broke my reverie to see if I might be of help. Lyle's Mom, Celia, had somehow misplaced her keys. Celia, whom I had met briefly over the winter as we came and went to piano, was calm and quiet as she began to go through her very full car. I offered to free eighteen-month-old Clemm from his car seat as his mother searched. I entered the toddler zone as we played ball, strolled through the grass on a key hunt, and Clemm offered me his luscious round self to hug.

The keys did not surface in the car. Lyle mentioned that he was missing his karate class—no anxiety, no whining, just observing. He then peacefully claimed his catcher's mitt and a ball from the belongings now piled on the sidewalk and found some kids to play catch.

"Mama" little Clemm repeated, pointing to his mother again and again, then "light" as he pointed to the light in the car, or the spotlight on a nearby building. This went on for over an hour. Celia, unflustered, retraced her steps, Lyle played a great game of catch, and Clemm pointed out lights then pointed to his "mama."

Elizabeth, finished with her lesson, joined us. Clemm pointed to her, then to me, and exclaimed "Mama." "Yes!" I practically leapt with joy at his connection, "I am her Mama." Just then the streetlight flickered on and Clemm shouted "light" as an enthusiastic preacher would shout "Alleluia."

I affirmed with Celia that all was in Divine order and that nothing was lost, misplaced, or stolen, in a perfect universe. We stood together for a moment with eyes closed and I imagined the light from that streetlight bathing us, two mothers, in grace.

I didn't get to my journal or my work but this lost key moving meditation filled me. I was awed by Celia's composure under duress and by her son's calm acceptance of the unexpected. I was inspired by Clemm's open, trusting, wise observations of mothers and light. I was honored to deliver this family to their home, knowing their keys would surely turn up and if not, there was a spare set at home.

As Mother's Day approaches we can be assured that we are indeed mothering in the light. Becoming a mother enriches our own spiritual life. We are stretched, in more ways than one, and changed after becoming mothers.

We are called on to juggle many balls, some of them crystal, some made of backyard mud. We can often feel as if we are whirling out of control. This fall I actually witnessed the Whirling Dervishes of Turkey perform a seven-hundred-year-old Islamic *sema* ceremony. White robed men spun their way to serenity in a form of moving contemplation. It all reminded me of the dance of motherhood. Rather than allowing the flurry of our everyday existence to knock us into a giddy response, it is possible to experience the serenity in the immediate.

The seemingly endless rotations of the Whirling Dervish dancers is symbolic of our days and nights as parents. When we raise our hopes, dreams, prayers, and needs to the heavens, as the dancers raise their palms to Allah, we are mothered, fulfilled, fed, tended to. We are grounded by our link with the Divine and anchored to an eternal sustaining light. We are spinning—but not out of control. We remain balanced when we lose our keys, are late for karate, or never get to the day's work quota.

My Mother's Day prayer for you is:

Just as the dancers maintain their physical axis, never getting dizzy, so do you remain centered and at peace. Your yearning for transcendence is quenched within the rhythm of your everyday life and you find the guiding light within to nourish and sustain you. Happy Mother's Day!

A mother is not a person to lean on but a person to make leaning unnecessary.

—DOROTHY CANFIELD FISHER

PARENTAL ENVY

I love the notion that it takes a village to raise a child, but lately I've been asking myself what kinds of adults inhabit this village. As children grow older, the intense pressure to accomplish increases. It's hard not to absorb this cultural craving for achievement—even though our heads tell us there's more to successful parenting then producing a wunderkind.

Many adults have a hard time celebrating the success of a child other than their own. It's as if John's lead in the school play is an affront to their child's acting skill. There is a rampant sense of comparison: "How did your daughter do on the math test?" "Was your son selected for the travel soccer team?" "My baby sleeps through the night—does yours?" Janet, mother of two children, wrote to me recently, describing her daughter's sixth-grade science fair as a testament to parental skill rather than evidence of any scientific learning on the part of many children.

Ten years ago, I wearily pushed my three-year-old in a swing at the local park, my one-week infant finally asleep in the Snugli. Next to me was a mother in the same situation. Her son strapped to her chest, her older child in the swing pumping to save her life. We made small talk about the safety of the old metal slide and our sleepless nights. I was shocked when this woman asked me, in a conspiratorial whisper, "What was your baby's APGAR score?" If this mother was already competitive about a newborn assessment test, I feel certain she is prepping her now-ten-year-old for the SATs—just to get a head start.

I've heard of parents who stop speaking to friends because of an altercation between their children. I wasn't surprised when the story came out a few years ago about the Texas cheerleader whose mother plotted to murder her teenage nemesis.

Kids can't help buying into their parents' envy of other children's positive qualities and successes. Teachers are swamped with complaints from parents who are angry about their child's lack of airtime in class. Coaches tell me that they are fed up with the parental pressure inflicted upon them. Stories of fourth and fifth graders sabotaging classmates' homework have crept into my inbox.

We are all connected. Let's begin to see the good in all kids and accept their strengths and talents as gifts that will make the world a better place instead of a threat to our child's success. The following are some ideas to strengthen the spiritual village in which your children are growing up and banish any parental envy creeping into your life:

BALANCING TIPS

—◌ Praise your children's friends—in front of your children. Mention their good qualities, rather than scanning them for weaknesses.

—◌ Applaud kids for kind actions, not just achievements. "Gee, I really liked the way you opened the door for all the kids coming in from recess."

—◌ Cut out the gossip—especially in front of your kids. Remember that gossip's purpose is to drag someone else down to make us feel better. I'm amazed at how often I hear adults engaging in negative talk

about their children's peers. Pull back and focus on the positive whenever the lure of gossip pulls you off balance.

— Pass along praise to children's parents. "I read about your daughter's art award. She's always had a gift for design. Congratulations!"
Doesn't it lift your heart to hear positive words about your child? Pass
it along with notes, e-mails, phone calls, and through conversation.

— It's one thing to applaud your child's accomplishments and quite
another to brag without a breath. The bumper sticker that notifies your
tailgaters that you've got an honor student in the family is fine as long
as you don't fall into the "My kid's better than your kid!" seductive
lure. Bragging about our child's incredible prowess is usually the desire
to alert the listener to our brilliant parenting. Straddle the line carefully between your own self-importance and supporting your child's
strengths. It's exhausting to always have to prove yourself. You'll find a
deeper sense of balance when you allow your child's strengths to shine
without having to tell the world.

— Mentor a child other than your own. This doesn't have to be a
formal arrangement. You might barter your skills with a neighbor—she
teaches your son chess and you spend time writing with her daughter.

— When envy surfaces, recognize and acknowledge it for what it
is—a wave of discontent and insecurity that causes us pain. Envy's
power is diffused when parent and child have a vocabulary for their
emotions. "When Sue gets all the attention from the teacher it makes
me feel bad." "When Maria's daughter was accepted at Harvard I
couldn't feel joy for her—only disappointment that my kid will never
have the grades for an Ivy League college."

—◦ "Gratitude" seems to be an overused word these days, but go ahead and overuse being thankful. When we are grateful for all the blessings in our lives, we shower ourselves in grace. A grateful heart minimizes envy and multiplies our gifts.

—◦ Remind yourself, and your kids, that there is enough good to go around. We live in a bountiful universe. We never miss out when we are balanced, remain true to ourselves, and follow our intuitive inner guidance. Envy, jealousy, and gossip knock us off that spiritual center.

Envy eats nothing but its own heart.

—GERMAN PROVERB

THE NO THAT CAN SAVE YOUR SOUL

Just today I've been asked to plan the annual trip for Whitney's class, lead tours for prospective parents at Elizabeth's school, set up for the youth theater's annual fund-raiser, organize publicity for an event, take part in an authors' festival at the local library, work at our town's spring festival, chaperone field trips at both daughters' schools, and bake for class night. And these are just community and school-related requests. Then there are the many requests we all receive every day in our careers and at home. "Will you . . . ," "Can you . . . ," "Do you mind . . . ," "Have you gotten to . . ." Where do we find room for ourselves amid this sea of appeals?

"No" is a small but powerful word that many of us, especially women, have a hard time saying, but in an attempt for calmer, more balanced lives, say it we must. For inspiration, just take a look at your toddler. She doesn't mince words and has no problem issuing a clear no. You will be more gracious, I'm sure, but giving yourselves permission to say no will give you the time and stamina you need to focus on what speaks to your heart.

Prioritizing your life will allow you to have control over your time and enable you to determine when to say yes and when to say no. If it's not high on your priority list, it doesn't make the cut. If you feel uncontrollable events steal your time, create an Ultimate Busy but Balanced list. Write down the priorities that are important to you. List your ten highest priorities as a parent and as a person on his or her own. Exercise and interaction with friends might give you the balance you seek, while someone else might need time for reading and gardening. Now when you are asked to do something, go to your list. If the request doesn't relate to your priorities, it's easy to say no. You'll stay focused, on target, and time will become your partner.

Lisa, mother of three, has a great analogy for prioritizing: "Only with years of practice have I learned how to say no. I realize that I have only a limited allotment of time and energy to spend each day, so I plan it the same way I do my financial budget. I plan before I go to bed each night how my time will be spent tomorrow. When anyone in my family has a special need, I tell others I cannot do this or that activity. I cannot make a commitment that I will be unable to keep. I cannot allow someone else to plan my time for me. I must know myself well enough to know when to stop, and I must have enough courage to take a stand for myself when my own needs are not being fulfilled."

Sometimes our kids can be our voice of reason. Jane is the mother of three and works part-time. She is one of the busiest women I know, filling every moment with an obligation. She says, "I'm not good at saying no, although I've narrowed my focus these days to one committee at church, PTA president at my kid's school, and, of course, my job.

My daughter did say to me recently, 'Oh please, Mama, don't do anything else.'"

Next time you are asked to volunteer your time, pause and listen to your inner voice. Weigh each request on a "how does it feel in my gut" scale. Then take a serenity scan to determine if saying yes will tip you off balance. Ask yourself, "Does the request I'm considering express more vitality in my life or zap my energy? How does the request fit into my family's priorities?" Jacob, father of three, says, "I say yes to what interests me or will really make a difference."

BALANCING TIPS

— Say no to gadgets you won't use and clothes you don't wear. There is room for serenity when we refuse to fill our homes with more physical objects. I have an electric ice-cream maker that we've used once over the past few years. It simply takes up precious cabinet space. I keep thinking it will come in handy some festive summer evening. The truth is, it's time to pass this contraption along to someone who really will whip up some mocha gelato and then invite us over to enjoy it.

— Practice the fine art of politely yet firmly saying no with telemarketers who call during dinnertime.

— Say no as a family. When you're clear on what your family believes in, then making decisions as a group becomes much easier. Melna has two children and very clear priorities: "Our Sabbath observance [Saturdays] ensures that we always spend that time together as a family. We never, ever (and I mean, never ever!) do anything on a Saturday that will mean one of us spending time elsewhere. That's our priority as a family."

—‍◌‍ Soften the blow of saying no by offering creative alternatives. Perhaps you could direct the person making the request to someone else who might be able to help out.

—‍◌‍ Think of your life as made up of time segments. There may be a portion of that time that you intend to tithe to something outside yourself that has meaning to you. Just as some people tithe 10 percent of their income, you might tithe 10 percent of your nonworking hours to something that moves you. This clear delineation of how you give your time makes responding to requests much easier. "Sorry, I've already filled my allotted volunteer time."

—‍◌‍ Prioritize all the many demands on your time by saying no to things without feelings. So if you have a free hour and your kitchen floor needs waxing but your teenager needs some time alone with you, pick your daughter over the floor.

—‍◌‍ Tell the truth. Don't get caught up in using lies to ease the impact of saying no. All sorts of complications will result, not the least of which is that your child will see lying as a way out of uncomfortable encounters.

—‍◌‍ Help kids learn to say no when they mean *no*. My daughter was asked to baby-sit for neighbors and friends soon after she turned twelve. She was busy with schoolwork and her many hobbies and yet felt guilty telling these families she couldn't spend time with their children. It was only after I explained that she didn't owe them an explanation, that she was better able to issue a blanket statement, "I'm sorry but I'm not able to baby-sit until this summer." What a relief for her.

—◦ If you aren't sure about a request, it's always okay to ask for time to think it over.

—◦ Often the toughest no is to those we love. If your child makes a request that you feel is over the top, it's in everyone's best interests to say no. Melaine is the single mom of David, age nine. She adores her son, tolerates her job as a nanny for four kids, and craves time for her own spirit. She told me, "I must be selfish sometimes with my time; otherwise I will be burnt out soon. So I explain to my son that he is my beloved one, but that he is not the only one in my life—that there is also me! I have interests and needs that I am not willing to suppress because if I did I would become ill and simply crazy."

> Do not think that love, in order to be genuine, has to be extraordinary. What we need is to love without getting tired.
>
> —MOTHER TERESA

> Stress is when your mind says no, but your mouth opens up and says yes.
>
> —ANONYMOUS

6

JUNE

SOULFUL FATHERING

The following tips for soulful fathering are in honor of Father's Day. Pass them along to your favorite dad. (Of course moms can use them, too.)

1. Listen to your heart when you are with your kids. Go with what feels right, not what your dad might have done or what you think fathers are *supposed* to do. You are the perfect match for your child. You can't make a mistake when you follow your intuitive guidance.
2. Share your hobbies with your kids.
3. Select one day a month or year to spend one-on-one time with each child. Mark the dates in your calendar. Let your child decide what the day's events will be and celebrate together!
4. Listen to your son or daughter. Playing catch is a wonderful time for listening.
5. The old saying "pick your battles" is an important one to remember. So what does it really matter if your son's clothing looks a little foolish—he's developing his own taste. Staying away from win-lose situations is much better in the long run for your relationship.
6. Don't forget the wonderful habit of note writing. Leave some unexpected words of encouragement in a book, under a pil-

low, via E-mail. If you travel, begin a postcard tradition. Send
your child a postcard from each trip you take.

7. Learn something new with your children.

8. Is there a way you might make some chore a ritual your child
looks forward to participating in with you? Maybe you wash
the windows every spring and then have an annual water fight.

9. Share your goals with your kids. Let them know how you have
achieved a dream and help them come up with an action plan
to achieve their own goals.

10. Don't forget the five "Ps" of fathering: Patience, Pure Love,
Playfulness, Participation, Persistence.

Remember, no one on their death bed ever said they wished they'd
spent more time at the office.

B A L A N C I N G   T I P

—◌ Think of your own father and how he showed his love to the
child you once were. Choose to celebrate his contribution to who you
are today or forgive his mistakes.

> *Across the field of yesterday*
> *he sometimes comes to me*
> *a little lad just back from play*
> *the lad I used to be.*
>
> —ANONYMOUS

TRANSITIONS AND TRADITIONS

When I was a little girl living in Mississippi, we celebrated the last day of school in a big way. My two brothers, sister, and I would gallop home, lugging our end-of-the-year treasures and proceed directly to the kitchen. We'd grab every pot, pan, wooden spoon, and lid we could find and dash outside to bang the lids, beat the spoons on the pans, and holler as loudly as possible. School was out and we marked the transition to "freedom" with a ruckus that shook the South.

Tomorrow is my daughter Elizabeth's last day of fourth grade. Banging pans doesn't really appeal to her and the "end of school parade" tradition we began years ago has fizzled out as a result of a mass exodus of school-age children from our neighborhood. I'm thinking of another way to mark the day—the transition to summer—with gusto. The problem? It's 8:00 P.M. and Whitney, my twelve year old, needs a little help determining if the egg whites are really stiff enough to create meringue for her science project due tomorrow. Our house is being painted, so it's tough to find the stove much less the mixer. I've got a radio interview in ten minutes, and it's a good thing listeners in thirty-eight states can't see my desk covered with the entire contents of our kitchen cabinets.

Our eight-year-old neighbor, who is staying for dinner, just shrieked from the bathroom that there isn't any toilet paper, and I know it's the same situation upstairs. Teacher's gifts have yet to be made, and I had better call to arrange for someone to care for the pets while we are out of town in . . . oh, yikes . . . two days.

Now is when I need to breathe deeply. Everyone reading this can join right along. With a collective breath we can center ourselves by pausing and going within, even amid what might feel like complete disorder.

Maybe our child's last day of school celebration won't be a bike parade with streamers and gaggles of kids but a quick trip to the ice-cream shop for a special sundae, or blowing up balloons in the backyard, or simply rolling down the car windows, honking the horn, and shouting, "Schools out for the summer." We have an annual tradition of stopping at the bookstore after the last day of school for the children to select a book to honor their year of learning and reading.

Elizabeth just announced that her stomach hurts, and she is sure she has salmonella poisoning (she rhymed it with vanilla) because she licked the beaters of her sister's meringue project . . . about ten egg whites ago.

Within the chaos that is often our lives with children, we can truly retreat, even for a moment, to that seed of serenity within. I'm finding it right now as I write this. Sometimes we just need a breath, a spiritual habit, a whispered prayer to remind us.

B A L A N C I N G   T I P S

—❦ Talk to kids about the ever present opportunity to renew themselves, without withdrawing from the world. It's as simple as pausing in the midst of their day and feeling the loving presence within or taking a deep breath and pretending they are filling their bodies with love and light.

—❦ Don't forget to reward yourself for another completed school year. All the homework help, driving, coordinating, planning, and packed lunches are over for a while. Have a long, hot soak in the tub, indulge in a peppermint hot fudge sundae, write the school year's highlights in your journal.

—◦ As this school year comes to a close, what tradition might your family begin? These "markers," silly as they might seem, are a real touchstone to the soul. Recognize the milestones in the lives of those you love with simple celebrations. Applaud their transitions, growth, and accomplishments. Remember, in the uncluttered life of a child, these are truly noteworthy events. Join in their excitement and watch as they bask in the recognition.

> *My parents always put a bouquet of flowers in my room on the first day of summer vacation. It makes me feel so great because even though I'm older now, I still feel sort of safe and like a kid again with that little tradition.*
>
> —AGE 13

LASTING PHOTOS

We miss many of the significant moments of our children's lives by trying to capture them on film. You've been there—rummaging through the camera bag for film, teetering in the overcrowded theater aisle, video camera blinking its obnoxious, red, low-battery light.

The alternative is "mental clicking." Pretend you have a mental photo album. This luminous collection of images from your life is tucked away in your consciousness. To add to your album you only need to "click." The baby is asleep in your arms, the summer breeze gently blowing her velvet tufts of hair, you are at peace, close your eyes and say "click"—freeze this moment.

"Click moments" are those times when you are awash with wonder, joy, bliss, or contentment. You can click your spiritual camera anytime—

you are gathered around the kitchen table with your happy, healthy family, your son comforts his sister who had a tough day at school, the puppy is curled up at your feet. Accept more of these moments into your life. Take your child's hand, point out simple magic moments, and click together.

Acknowledging the beauty and gifts we receive each day opens the flow for more good to reveal itself. "Clicking" is a habit that freezes those sparkling moments that, linked together, become the scrapbook of our lives.

BALANCING TIP

Begin today to accept more good than you experienced yesterday. Talk to your child about "click moments" and be on the lookout for a few this weekend.

Life gives; we must receive it.
—ERNEST HOLMES

LANGUAGE OF THE SOUL

Prayer is a concrete way to affirm our spirituality, to put our worries, hopes, affirmations, quandaries, and joys out on the table. It's a path toward deeper intimacy with God and with our family. When we pray together, we move toward spirit as a unit—we pause and breathe in the rejuvenating grace—together. Prayer is a natural forum for linking our humanness with the healing energy of the universe. By sharing this discovery with our children, we give them a powerful tool for life. When we invoke the presence of God, our lives become more meaningful, ordinary moments more sacred. Once we resolve to create a meaningful life for our family—prayer, no longer a static concept, becomes a natural way to reach toward the Divine together.

Many of us are frantically managing hectic schedules, trying to make a living, juggling divorce consequences, helping kids with homework, going back to school ourselves, assisting elderly parents, dealing with behavior issues; we have little time for a leisurely telephone chat, much less adding prayer to our "To Do" list. The truth is, once we pause, take a breath, and become quiet, we realize that even with all the activity there is a loneliness, a longing, a thirst for something more meaningful—both for us and for our kids. A spiritual practice that links us to a loving Presence and to our family can assuage that longing—not to mention make all the other parts of our lives fall into place easily—with less strain and more delight. No religious training or dogmatic rules are necessary to begin praying, only the desire to put oneself in the spiritual flow.

Prayer is not limited to old associations with meaningless words we may have been made to memorize as children. Nor is it defined by the 1950s image of a white family gathered around the fire praying the rosary with bowed heads. Instead, prayer can become a vibrant, integral, alive part of any family. We can dance our prayers, sing our prayers, think our prayers, breathe our prayers, walk our prayers, hum our prayers, paint our prayers, be our prayers in action. Prayer can be a poem about the stunning majesty of a waterfall or a child's simple rhyme about Mother Earth. We can pray in the bathtub, on the way to work, on the soccer field, in our journals, or on our morning walk.

As I work with children and their parents, I find the words they use to pray as varied as their needs. Often the most poignant words are those that come from children directly. "God, You are the best in the world," spoken by an eight year old in glee feels pretty great shouted by a thirty-eight year old. No matter our age, we can claim and craft a unique style of praying.

To infuse our family with spirit, we can begin to articulate our hopes, dreams, wishes, longings, blessings through prayer—separately and together. Fleeting words spoken together before the start of a busy workday can carry us through with grace. Repeating a familiar prayer can be just the balm to soothe a worried nine year old as she faces her first big test. Posting a favorite saying on the refrigerator can remind us to silently affirm the words as we go about our kitchen routine. Ending our days by gathering together for a moment of "grateful prayers" before heading upstairs to bed can remind us of the good in our lives and end the day on a positive note.

One family I know has incorporated prayer into their busy sports routine. As their three kids head off to a practice or game, they use the time in the car to pray for protection, Divine order, and fun on the field. Another mother of three looks forward to the blissful moment when her kids are in bed and she can make the rounds to read a prayer with each child—the child selects the prayer from a tattered notebook of favorites they have compiled.

Mealtime is prayer time for many families. The hustle and bustle of active lives are, for a moment, quiet as all are seated and many variations of prayers are celebrated. One family raises their hands and their voices to shout, "Hip, hip, hooray," before lifting their forks. My daughter asked for a Quaker blessing the other night. We held hands, closed our eyes, and instead of our usual out loud prayers that go around the table, we were silent, each person reflecting privately. Of course action quickly picked up after our instant of quiet, but it was a centering moment that brought us all to the present.

Prayer is joy, gratitude, loving intentions, peace, and delight. It is a dynamic tool for creating sacred times in the life of a family—a foundation for family spirit.

You might want to write or type the following prayers on index cards for your child. He can add his own prayers as they occur to him.

I am a most important person to God
for I am God in action.
God listens through my ears
speaks through my words
and reaches out through my touch.
I celebrate God when I celebrate me.

I love being alive.

I can have all I imagine and expect.
I take the words "I can't" right out of my vocabulary.
No more "buts" and lots more "I can's."
I stay awake to my God potential.

God is love and I am one with God.

As I look out my window and see
Looking out my window is looking into me
I am slow to anger
Full of love
Knowing God is by my side

—AGE 10

I am thankful for this beautiful morning
The blue sky

The green grass
For the sunlight beginning to creep in.

—AGE 7

When the mind knows, we call it knowledge.
When the heart knows, we call it love.
When the being knows, we call it prayer.

—ANONYMOUS

HELPING KIDS MANAGE FEAR

The powerful web of fear can envelop us and zap our natural spontaneity and joy at any age. Many young kids struggle with vivid, fearful pictures springing from their imaginations. As they grow older, their fears grab at them in different ways. They become fearful of the world through stories they hear, television shows they watch, real situations they encounter.

When our children experience fear, worry, and anxiety let's listen to them, believe them, have a discussion, and then gently guide them to solutions.

The following ideas can help children manage their struggles with fear.

BALANCING TIPS

—↶ Encourage your child's relationship with God. When she turns trustingly to God, a child can share worries she might not be able to discuss with parents or friends. There is a certain wonderful safety in knowing "God won't tell." God is flexible and can become anything a child might need at any given time. This personalized Divine Spark meets kids exactly where they are each moment. An anxious nine year old said, "God is like a blaze of power in my heart. When I need that power, I just feel it." For a seventeen year old, "God is a loving presence when I get scared."

—☙ Find a talisman that's comforting to your child, such as a picture of Mary, Jesus, Buddha, angels, a unicorn, a sunset, and let her carry it in a pocket during the day or put it under a pillow at night. Relics, rocks, medals, and home altars are comforting, concrete objects that can be used to gain inner serenity and peace.

—☙ When my kids experience anxiety before some major event, such as the first day of school, performing in a play, or a big test, I remind them to breathe. Most of us hold our breath when we are locked in fear, and just shifting our attention to breathing helps dissipate anxiety.

—☙ If your child is afraid to go to sleep, find specific images to ease her into dreamland. One five-year-old girl imagined angels flying around the room keeping the monsters away: "My angel is a pretty butterfly. She helps me fall asleep when I have a hard time. She has beautiful colors around her—like stained glass."

—☙ Help your children confront scary incidents by equipping them with knowledge. When fear is aroused by a specific event, such as a big lightning storm or a loud, barking dog, information and facts can empower kids.

⟶ Very young children use make-believe to "become" what they fear in order to manage it. They may pretend to be growling dogs, one-eyed monsters, gruff doctors, or roaring lions, and meet their fears vicariously while gaining a sense of control over their world. Give your kids enough free playtime to organize their fears and conquer them.

⟶ Brainstorm with your child about ways to manage his fears. Often just by sitting down and taking the time to imagine options, your child will come up with his own unique and powerful solutions, as did this six year old: "When scary pictures come in my head—like a witch, a monster, or our house burning down—I pretend it's from a photo album and I turn the pages until I get to a picture I like."

⟶ Be conscious of the media messages children take in. Television news and scary movies, with their violent images, aren't appropriate for children under ten. Even older kids suffer when barraged with anxiety-producing content.

TELL THE TRUTH—THE WHOLE TRUTH

Cheating, lying, and deceiving are unattractive spirit-squashing traits, to be sure. The very words sound sordid and dark and way beyond our lives. Yet kids lie. And kids hear their parents lie. Often kids are nurtured in an uneven emotional environment where lies, evasions, and double messages are the rule. We don't mean to be a model of dishonesty, but habits are hard to break.

When we lie we create distance between ourselves and the person we've lied to, we shift into a dishonest relationship without authentic connection. It's difficult for soulful growth or balance to occur in an atmosphere of distrust.

CHARACTER COUNTS! Coalition took a national survey of high school students. I was more than dismayed with the results: Ninety-two percent had lied to their parents in the past twelve months (79 percent said they had done so two or more times); 78 percent had lied to a teacher (58 percent two or more times); more than one in four (27 percent) said they would lie to get a job.

Cheating, another form of dishonesty, is rampant. Seventy-one percent of all high school students admit they had cheated on an exam at least once in the past twelve months (45 percent said they had done so two or more times).

I did an informal study of my own. I spoke with kids of all ages over the past few weeks about lying. Here's the essence I gleaned of why so many are not telling the truth:

- Kids don't want to let their parents down. They feel an enormous pressure to live up to the high expectations their family has for them. Lying is often easier than disappointing Mom and Dad.
- Fear of punishment is a big incentive for kids to lie.
- Lying doesn't really matter they think. What difference does it make if I tell a lie?
- Older kids use lying as a way to seek revenge against "the system."
- Some kids lie because that's what they hear at home. They use lying to get out of jams because it's what they've seen their parents do.
- Many kids have admitted that telling a small lie is a way to test the waters, to gain independence. It's almost a natural part of rebelling, of pushing boundaries.

- There is a fine line between exaggerating and lying, and many kids continue to broaden that line.
- And for some children, lying is a way to finally get their parent's attention. "I hate school, the teacher has it in for me."

When our kids lie, an emotional minefield is ignited for many of us. We might recall shame-filled and punishment-ridden religious teachings of our youth. We never imagined our beloved child deceiving us—we have taught them it's wrong. Haven't we?

Sara, mother of three, writes: "My son told me a lie over a year ago (he was 6) and the most painful thing about the experience still is that I knew instantly that he was lying because he was afraid of what I would do if he told the truth.

"As gently as I could I walked him through the process of getting through the fear of telling the truth. When we finished talking, he understood that there would be consequences for the original action that inspired the lying, but that I would not be angry if he told the truth but quite the opposite: I would applaud the difficult task of truth telling. He hasn't (knock on wood) told a lie since."

To foster a sense of truthfulness in your children try the following tips:

BALANCING TIPS

◦ We can begin by making sure home is a safe place. Kids usually lie when they are afraid to tell the truth.

⌒ It's a developmental certainty that young children will lie. "I didn't hit her." "No, I didn't eat the candy." Address it right away. Look deeply into your child's eyes and firmly let him know, "We don't tell lies. Lying isn't okay." Help your children understand early on how your family communicates: "Our family believes in honesty and speaking the truth."

⌒ We can do the courageous and difficult work of becoming honest in our own lives. We need to be honest with our children and especially with ourselves. We teach by what we do. Stop telling small white lies to get yourself out of uncomfortable situations. "You didn't get that paperwork? Gee, that's odd because I sent it last week." Be truthful and your child will see how you take responsibility. "I'm sorry. I should have sent the papers but I just haven't gotten to it. I will Federal Express them out today at my own expense."

⌒ Being loved and feeling a connectedness with others, especially one's parents, is absolutely vital to kids—even more than being punished. So when that closeness is at stake, the practical implications don't much matter. A lie is minor next to losing the love of your sole "soul" provider. Make sure you are loving and honoring your children, not just managing their lives and delivering rules and consequences.

⌒ Lies become habitual. Stop them when they start by instituting deep and honest communication. Consider sharing the Character Counts statistics (above) with your child and use the study to spark conversation about this topic.

⌒ Come up with ways to let your child have some control over her life and rebel without resorting to lying. Give your child alternatives.

Gayle, mother of eight-year-old Samantha, said, "I asked my daughter if she had brushed her teeth this morning. She said she had. I looked closer and responded, "Sam, you did not brush your teeth, did you?" She giggled as if she had done something cute. I said, "Look, you can be angry at me, you can stamp your feet, but you can't lie to me."

—⌒ It can be humiliating when our child lies publicly, but let's get over our own egos and ensure our child takes responsibility and faces his mistakes. Kathy, mother of seven-year-old Luke, was horrified when his teacher phoned to say Luke had called another child a racist name. Luke denied it to his mother, so she went to bat for him. Ultimately, Luke told the truth. He had indeed called the child by this name. His parents were mortified, but they insisted Luke write a letter of apology to the child, the child's parents, his teacher, and even the school principal to apologize for wasting everyone's time with this incident.

> *Adults find pleasure in deceiving a child. They consider it necessary, but they also enjoy it. The children very quickly figure it out and then practice deception themselves.*
>
> —ELIAS CANETTI

STRENGTHENING SIBLING TIES

Enough about sibling rivalry! What about strengthening sibling ties? When we focus on the negative in any relationship, that's just what we get. The term *sibling rivalry* has become a mantra for many exasperated parents. We almost expect kids to compete for our attention, bicker, and tattle on each other. No family is without a certain amount of discord. But what if we focused on creating a sibling "team" rather than putting out the fires of sibling rivalry?

Children's relationships with each other have a significant impact on who they are to become. If you take a moment and think back to your own childhood and how you related to your sisters and brothers, what surfaces? How did your parents treat sibling issues? Do you wish they had done something differently? Our memories of sibling relationships profoundly affect how we empower our own kids to handle sibling confrontations.

Are you aware of how your children really feel about one another? Take the next week to observe their relationship with a loving heart. Stay open to how you can create an atmosphere of collaboration in your home. Cooperation makes family life run smoother and allows positive feelings to flow more fully.

BALANCING TIPS

— Encourage your kids to work as a team. Suggest they make pizza together every Sunday night, or put them in charge of recycling bottles and deciding how the return money is spent.

— Step back and allow your children to create their own relationships apart from you. Catch yourself if you tend to micromanage their interactions.

— When kids begin to squabble, don't become the referee. Come up with ways they can work out their own spats. If you are looming at

the ready, they will compete for your approval. One mother I know
does more than just send fighting kids to their rooms. She asks them to
stand in their bedroom doorways and talk out the problem. They aren't
to return downstairs until they have worked it out. Standing in the
doorway staring at each other leads to lots of interesting solutions—all
without parental input.

—❧ Spend equal one-on-one time with each child. This communicates, "Yes, we are a team, but you are special!" We all want to be loved
for our unique selves.

—❧ Part of being in a relationship is having disagreements, feeling
irritation, and getting angry. Our kids feel all these emotions intensely.
The key is to accept that negative feelings will surface and have a built-
in structure for dealing with them. Our reaction to children's fighting
is also natural. One father of two literally saw red when his kids began
arguing. It was important for him not to become embroiled in his kids'
disagreements but to step back and analyze why the fighting began.
Were the children tired, frustrated, overstimulated?

—❧ Just because children are born into the same family doesn't
guarantee they will adore one another. We can't force kids to be best
friends. We can, however, create a noncompetitive atmosphere and a
soulful home. When we don't expect automatic "brotherly love," we
can lessen the guilt associated with, "Well, he's your brother, you
should love him."

—❧ Take time to truly observe each of your children to discover
their temperament and approach to the world. What makes their spirits sing?

—☙ Strive to meet a child's individual need when it arises. When one child is sick, he may need chicken soup and a back massage. That doesn't mean it's unfair that his sister doesn't get the special treatment. Her turn will come.

—☙ It's our job to care for our children. Never expect an older sister or brother to baby-sit without asking.

Resources

PART TWO: SPRING

Adult Books

Cameron, Julia. *The Artist's Way*. New York: Jeremy P. Tarcher/Putnam, 1995. A classic creativity opener. Julia just knows how to get us to open to that rich vein of inspiration running through our souls.

Doe, Mimi, and Marsha Walch. *10 Principles for Spiritual Parenting*. New York: HarperCollins, 1998. If you want more hands-on, action-based ideas on how to keep your child's natural spirit alive and nourished, this is your book. What a joy it was to work on this book with my mom, Marsha Walch.

Dunn, Philip. *Prayer: Language of the Soul*. New York: Daybreak Books, 1997. These collected prayers and reflections from around the world will speak to your entire family.

Lawlor, Anthony. *A Home for the Soul*. New York: Clarkson Potter, 1997. The beautiful photographs alone make me feel soulful.

Madden, Chris Casson. *A Room of Her Own: Women's Personal Spaces*. New York: Clarkson Potter, 1997. I felt renewed just gazing at these beautiful images of private, inspiring spaces.

Ponder, Catherine. *The Dynamic Laws of Prayer*. Marina del Rey, CA: DeVorss, 1962. The wording can sound a bit dated but the message and the ideas are truly miraculous.

Reeves, Judy. *A Writer's Book of Days, A Spirited Companion & Lively Muse for the Writing Life,* San Rafael, CA: New World Library, 1999. Another resource to prompt you to put pen to paper.

Spade, Deborah. *Teaching Your Kids to Care.* New York: Citadel Press, 1995. This book is full of great ideas on how to empower kids to reach out.

Kids

Cooney, Barbara. *Roxaboxen.* New York: Lothrop, Lee and Shepard Books, 1991. This book reminds us of the importance of imagination and free time. It's about children creating their own world.

Handford, Martin. *Where's Waldo?* Cambridge, MA: Candlewick Press, 1997. Have fun with this entire series of books. Tune into your intuition for a real experience.

Kubler Ross, Elizabeth. *Remember the Secret.* Berkeley, CA: Celestial Arts, 1998. A beautiful story for young children by our leading authority on death and dying, Elizabeth Kubler Ross.

Rylant, Cynthia. *The Heavenly Village.* New York: The Blue Sky Press, 1999. I love anything Cynthia Rylant has written, but this book is particularly poignant for all ages.

————. *Missing May.* New York: Dell Yearling, 1992. May dies and Ob misses her so much that he considers trying to contact her. Instead, he reaches out and connects with those around him. I was reading this book, coincidentally, when my father died. They were just the words I needed to read.

Shriver, Maria. *What's Heaven?* New York: St. Martin's Press, 1999. Parents are often stumped when their children ask questions about heaven. This book takes the words right out of your mouth.

Waldman, Jackie. *Teens with the Courage to Give.* Berkeley, CA: Conari Press, 2000. When Elizabeth finished this inspiring little book, all in one sit-

ting, her response was, "Mom, kids really can change the world." One
girl who was profiled says, "The courage to give is the fuel to live."
Pretty incredible role models, I'd say.

Web Sites

www.familycares.org. Full of great ideas for reaching out as a family.
www.Beliefnet.com. A wonderful site with segmented content for all
faiths.
www.couragetogive.com. The companion site to *The Courage to Give* book
series.
www.charactercounts.org. This site is devoted to the work of Character Counts
and includes wonderful resources any family, school, or organization
can use.

Magazines

intuition magazine. www.intuitionmagazine.com. 415-538-8171 Open to
yours and your life will never be the same. True balance comes from
diving into your intuitive knowing and following it.

Prayer Lines

There's a wonderful belief that individuals united in prayer create a powerful force, the power of the group squared. The following listings are
organizations dedicated to focusing light and energy on the prayer
requests of anyone who calls. The volunteers are truly amazing. Leave
these numbers around for your older children. I've know a few teens
who have found enormous comfort from speaking to an anonymous
prayer person.

Association for Research and Enlightenment
215 Sixty-seventh Street
Virginia Beach, VA 23451
800-333-4499
757-428-3588 (x7551)

Science of Mind World Ministry of Prayer
3251 West Sixth Street
Los Angeles, CA 90020-5096
800-421-9600
213-385-0209

Silent Unity
Unity Village, MO 64065-0001
800-669-7729
816-969-2026 (Spanish)

Television and Radio

www.odysseychannel.com. Odyssey Network, 800-841-8476. Yes, there is
positive programming available on television. Odyssey has cornered
the market on creating and delivering soul-nourishing shows via their
twenty-four-hour cable channel.
WISDOM Radio and WISDOM Television, www.wisdomradio.com. The
menu of spiritual programming is increasing monthly. Check the Web
site to find out how to find both the television and radio shows that will
enhance your life.
"The Tony Trupiano Show" on *Talk America*. Tony's show is fantastic and will
surely help you balance your life. He reaches about eighty-three mar-
kets in the United States and airs at 6:00–8:00 P.M. EST. You can also

listen live on the Internet by going to www.talkamerica.com then
clicking on Talk2.

Music

Halpern, Steven. "Gifts of the Angels." www.stevenhalpern.com. What
delicious, relaxing music. Turn off the lights, turn on this CD, and hold
your child in your arms while the choir of angels lulls your to bliss.

PART THREE

SUMMER

Lemonade on the back porch, chasing fireflies with a gaggle of kids, a cool dip in the silent pond, reading an inspiring book in the shady hammock, a car trip to a new destination. What summer memories do you want to create for your family? It is possible to weave old-fashioned summer joys into your fast-paced modern life—it just takes some thought and planning. Slow down and listen to the song of summer that's waiting for you to turn up the volume. ⟿

7

JULY

WHAT'S WORKING NOW?

As we enter July, halfway through the year, it's a great time to do a quick life scan. How are your days flowing? Are you satisfied with the current circumstances in your life? Is there a particular area that needs attention?

Take the following Balance Barometer when you have some time to reflect. The results will help you refocus and hone in on what areas need attention in order to experience more balance in your life.

Balance Barometer

T F

☐ ☐ I get between eight and ten hours of sleep a night.
☐ ☐ I usually wake up feeling positive about the day ahead.
☐ ☐ I have enough time with my children.
☐ ☐ I have enough time with my partner.
☐ ☐ I have enough time for myself.
☐ ☐ I have enough time for my career.
☐ ☐ I feel loved and cherished.
☐ ☐ My home feels organized most of the time.
☐ ☐ There is beauty around me in my home.

☐ ☐   I earn what I deserve.

☐ ☐   I have six to nine months of living expenses in liquid savings.

☐ ☐   I have begun a college savings plan for my children.

☐ ☐   I have begun a retirement savings plan for myself.

☐ ☐   My will and guardian decisions for my kids are in order.

☐ ☐   I am recognized for my accomplishments.

☐ ☐   I have a spiritual practice that nourishes my soul.

☐ ☐   My spouse and I are in agreement about our children's spiritual development.

☐ ☐   I feel connected to my family.

☐ ☐   I feel connected with a community of some sort.

☐ ☐   I have a close friend I speak with often.

☐ ☐   I am within five pounds of my ideal weight.

☐ ☐   I eat healthy meals most of the time.

☐ ☐   I watch television less than seven hours a week.

☐ ☐   There are many more accomplishments I hope to have but I am at peace with the core of my life.

☐ ☐   I joyfully anticipate the future.

1–2 False: Bravo! You have taken control of the details of your life and are satisfied with your current circumstances. You have created a solid structure for your family so that you can approach the rest of the year with joyful expectation.

3–5 False: Create a plan for approaching loose ends. You're more than halfway there. You'll find lots more energy once you've attended to the "undone" list.

6+ False: You are dissatisfied with how your life is working. Now is the time to take control of circumstances so they don't control you.

Make a commitment to create more balance in the second half of the year by taking action on at least one item from the above list.

FREEDOM

If you live in the United States, use the celebration of Independence Day as an opportunity to acknowledge your freedom to be all you came to this earth to be.

When your son exclaims over the dramatic fireworks display, remind him that he, too, is free to demonstrate a spectacular life. He is fueled by a light more powerful than those in the sky tonight. This constant inner light, spirit guiding him, is the launching pad for his every need.

Just as the artist chooses which colors to use in each fireworks design, so, too, can your child select his actions. He can choose to forgive his sister and release the suffocating pull of anger. She can decide to give field hockey a try and do her best while on the field, picturing herself as a strong defensive player enjoying the teamwork.

Use the Fourth of July to shake yourself free from limiting thoughts, judgments, and dis-ease. Celebrate your independence from useless fears and constraints that hold you back. You will then illustrate a parent who is free to express the miracle of who he or she is, not limited by outside circumstances.

And what is it but fragments of your own self you
would discard that you may become free?

—KAHLIL GIBRAN

SUMMER RHYTHM

It's summertime and the living should be a little easier. Have you down-shifted your rhythm into a slower pace? When you think of summer, what comes to mind? Catching minnows at the local pond? Licking an ice-cream cone with your dad? Take time out for activities reminiscent of your childhood and create some new summer rituals with your kids. The child in you will squeal with glee, and the child who lives with you will squeal right along.

Sprinkle some of the following ideas into your balmy summer days:

B A L A N C I N G   T I P S

—⟡ Dedicate a day in June as "Strawberry Day." The week before your juicy day, grab a big canvas bag and head out to the children's section at your local library for books with a strawberry theme. A few to get you started:

The First Strawberries : A Cherokee Story by Joseph Bruhac; *Flicka, Ricka, Dicka and the Strawberries* by Maj Lindman; *The Grey Lady and the Strawberry Snatcher* by Molly Bang; *The Little Mouse, the Red Ripe Strawberry, and the Big Hungry Bear* by Don and Audrey Wood.

Peek into the adult section for some strawberry recipe books. Try: *Cooking with Strawberries* by Margaret and Virginia Clark or *Strawberry Shortcake:A Recipe Collection Using the Strawberry, Naturally, in All of Its Forms* by Susan A. McCreary.

Now you're ready to go strawberry picking. Check your local paper for farms that have a "Pick Your Own." Lather on sunscreen and don your favorite straw hats. When you've filled your baskets, rush home to bake some pound cake or make some jam. What a strawberry feast you'll have. You might just launch an annual Strawberry Day tradition in your family.

—᷎ Let your kids loose in the kitchen to invent their own concoctions. Maybe they could create a portable summer menu using fruit on a stick, sandwiches, crackers and peanut butter—then pack it all up for an evening picnic dinner. One mother waits all year for summertime cooking with her kids: "I take two weeks off each summer to relax with my four children. We plan summer feasts in the cold winter months. We don't go away on a fancy vacation, but we pretend we're at the shore with our lobster bakes and in a Parisian café sipping iced tea. My kids are young, but they know how to peel ginger and giggle over kitchen adventures."

—᷎ How about high tea this afternoon? Tea doesn't have to be taken indoors, and the guests don't have to be real people. Do your kids know who began the tradition of afternoon tea? It was Duchess Anna Bedford, who just couldn't wait until dinner to eat.

—᷎ Any chance you have a young journalist living in your house? Encourage her to turn off the television and grab a notebook—your neighborhood needs a neighborhood newspaper. Maybe she has a few pals living nearby who could help. Your young journalist might start with a pet listing so neighbors become familiar with the cocker spaniels, golden retrievers, and mutts living nearby. Is there something of historical note in your neighborhood? Your child might interview home owners to find out about the lore associated with their homes or the ghosts who live in their attics. Support your child's efforts by typing, copying, or distributing the first edition.

—⌒ Set up a game table on your porch, deck, or under a shady tree—a simple card table will do. Buy a large, plastic, waterproof bin with a snug top to store puzzles, games, and a deck of cards. Maybe your house will be known as the "place to stop for a good game of chess or checkers."

—⌒ Head over to a local pond or lake at sunset (imagine it's Walden Pond) and read some of Thoreau's writings. Children are able to understand so many of his simple yet wise thoughts. A great place to begin is this line from *Consciousness in Concord:* "Any melodious sound apprises me of the infinite wealth of God." You can listen to the melodious sounds of God all around you. Or how about the following from Thoreau's journal, dated June 22, 1852: "Is not the rainbow a faint vision of God's face? How glorious should be the life of man passed under this arch! What more remarkable phenomenon than a rainbow, yet how little it is remarked!"

Return to the pond, each with a journal, and write your own esoteric thoughts.

—⌒ Don't take butterflies for granted—any creature that smells stuff with their feet is pretty cool. Gardens, meadows, fields, and woods are great places for spotting these beautiful nectar feeders. Is there milkweed growing in a vacant lot near your home? If so, it's a sure bet your kids will find some Monarchs. Read up on butterflies. *North America's Favorite Butterflies* by Patti and Milt Putnam is just the right size for little hands. Bring a sketch pad to draw the varieties you see: Mourning Cloak, American Lady, Painted Lady, Gray Hairstreak, or Great Spangled Fritillary.

—⌒ Select one state a week and focus your reading, games, songs, and words on that state. Scholastic's *The Kids' Book of the 50 Great States*

and Harry N. Abrams's detailed *Art of the State* series should
helpful. If this week is Mississippi week, how about cooking up some
shrimp scampi and learning about gators or kudzu?

—☙ Don't forget the magical summer ritual of freezing fruit juice
into Popsicles. Add a little surprise by dropping a tiny piece of fruit
into the bottom of one of the paper cups before freezing. Who will be
the lucky recipient of the fruit pop? That person is then responsible for
selecting the ingredients for the next batch of Popsicles.

> *Talking to my flowers in the morning is my solu-*
> *tion to the "gotta water the garden" chore. I greet*
> *them as I would a cherished group of friends. "Good*
> *morning, girls, how did you sleep?" Then I've nur-*
> *tured myself, my friends the flowers, and I've had*
> *some quiet time before the kids awake.*
>
> —BONNIE, MOTHER OF TWO

WATCH ME, MOM

My mother used to say, "For such a little girl, you're so loud." And being
a middle child I used that vocal capacity to its full extent. Standing on
the diving board of our backyard pool I would yell, "Watch me, Mama!"
again and again. My own children shout the same pool-side pleas.
"Watch this! Judge my dive! Guess who I am? Watch me, Mom!"

This hunger for mother's eyes, parental approval, doesn't go away. I
still call my mom with any sliver of good news. "Watch me, Mama.
How am I doing? Applaud me." And if we turn away, too busy to watch,

pretty soon our children resign themselves to our absence and stop calling to us.

Kids' shouts of, "Watch me, Mom!" shift as they grow older to, "Notice me, friends!" then, "Acknowledge me, world!" How is your child calling to you, to his or her friends, to the world? Do you need to create more time and space to hear your beloved son or daughter?

BALANCING TIP

Imagine your child on a diving board, arms open, knees shivering, yelling for your attention. His or her high voice carries across the summer breeze. "Watch me, Mom!" "Hey, Dad, look at this!" Now notice him, applaud her.

> *When you plant lettuce, if it does not grow well, you don't blame the lettuce. You look for reasons it is not doing well. It may need fertilizer, or more water, or less sun. You never blame the lettuce. Yet if we have problems with our friends or our family, we blame the other person. But if we know how to take care of them, they will grow well, like the lettuce. Blaming has no positive effect at all, nor does trying to persuade using reason and argument. That is my experience. If you understand, and you show that you understand, you can love, and the situation will change.*
>
> —THICH NHAT HANH

TOUGH TIMES

We all experience difficult times in our parenting—throughout the day and over the years. These are the times we aren't in harmony with our child. We're out of step and somehow disconnected. It helps, during these phases, to back off for a moment and love the essence of your child, his or her beautiful inner being. Kids, like all of us, go in and out of stages when they try on new behavior or work out some particular issue. When they have had a bad day, we are their safest outlet. It can be trying, exhausting, annoying, upsetting, and frightening to remain connected and love the child you know is behind the unappealing behavior. It's better to be compassionate rather than to be right, and to send love directly from your heart to your child's.

Go to a quiet place and pray, ask for insight and guidance on how best to reach the glimmer inside your beloved but obnoxious child. Don't allow yourself to become sucked into the whining, the fear, the worry, the faultfinding, the victim, the sick tummy, whatever your child is choosing to display to "get to you." Rise above the surface and continue to love and send light to the soul within.

Of course there are limits to unpleasant behavior, and respect for each member of the family is essential. But think back to your own childhood and all you did to explore your essential self apart from your parents. Let's remember to love our children through their phases and, rather than pull away and retreat from this seemingly new person, forge a new path to support and love them as they are.

B A L A N C I N G   T I P S

⁓☙ Try holding your child in the light of the new day. Focus on him as pure spirit—without yesterday's impressions to define him. Come forward into your relationship as if it were a complete surprise, not bound by the past.

⁓☙ Peek in on your sleeping child no matter her age. Sometimes all those warm, fuzzy love feelings come wafting back when we gaze upon an angelic sleeping face.

⁓☙ If you are part of a parenting group, rely on other members as sounding boards, a support team, and idea generators for the dilemmas you face at home. It's often the advice and wisdom of fellow parents that offer us just the glimmer we need to solve a problem or make a change. "What worked for our family was . . ." "You might try . . ." "When my daughter was going through a similar experience we . . ."

> *For it seems the way of Nature that any age of balanced equilibrium in the child's life needs to be followed by an age of marked disequilibrium.*
>
> —LOUISE BATES AMES, PH.D.

INTUITIVE TRAVEL

As my family and I set off for our one-week holiday, we agreed to collect life stories as our souvenirs. We could be fully present to all that was around us and open our hearts to connect with others placed on our path when dinner was cooked by someone else, homework was history, and there were no calls to return.

The children were intrigued by the idea that everyone we met had a life story—the waiter, Edward, who promised to visit on his November vacation, the cab driver we ran into again and again in a little French village, the sisters we met in a train station then again in a market hundreds of miles away; the gentleman seated next to us on the plane traveling to America from India for the first time; the large family from Holland gathered for a family wedding, who included us in their joy.

We experienced a kind of holiness in our encounters because our intention was to consider more than just surface interactions. We were able to hear our inner voices because our lives were turned down—and hear them we did. One morning, after checking out of our bed-and-breakfast and heading on to our next destination, something told me to check for our passports. Sure enough, I had been so busy making plans with our new French friends for their daughter to visit us next summer that I had left the passports and all our money lying on the kitchen table. Only five minutes out of town, we quickly turned back. If I hadn't acted upon my gut feeling, our trip would have unraveled in a different direction.

"Let's turn up this street and see where it leads," urged Whitney, and there before us lay a magical winding lane.

"I feel as if we should turn around and get the car rather than walk," sighed Elizabeth, as we hiked to see ancient huts. Sure enough, the distance was much greater than we had anticipated and driving allowed us to happily experience the rest of the day.

Life was simple and sweet during our time away. How, I wondered, might I recreate some of that moment-by-moment awareness, that awake-to-everything-around-us sensation, that trust of intuition, that connection with others, right here in our own small town, in our ordinary family life? How might I extend our vacation awareness and closeness?

Here are some ideas I came up with. Join me in trying them. Summer is the perfect time to shift gears and experience the ordinary in a whole new light. Happy intuitive traveling, whether you journey out or explore your own front yard.

B A L A N C I N G   T I P S

—✑ Select a day to visit your town as if for the first time. Forget chores and routines and instead strap the binoculars around your neck and head out to explore. Read some local history, eat lunch in a restaurant you've never tried, ask for directions even if you know where you're going. Take the time to talk to the waitress, speak to the family next to you in the park, and open your awareness to guide you on your explorations.

—✑ When we focus on reaching out to others, it takes us up and out of our own egos. It's further evidence that we're all connected and all life has a purpose. Let's encourage kids to operate with safety but to ask questions and share in the stories of those who pass through their lives. We show them by example how it's done.

—✑ Being away from routines and household distractions can bring siblings closer together. Plan a day or two away from home—just the family and very little agenda. Try to let go of any preconceived notion of how kids will act.

—◦ Eat outside during these summer nights and extend mealtime with candles, conversation, and that lingering vacation feel.

—◦ Recognize the holy beneath the surface of everyone you meet. Ask your child to see the sacred nugget within the bus driver, the camp counselor, the irritating kid down the street.

—◦ On our trip we stayed in an old cloister converted into a hotel. By chance, the room we were given had once been a chapel. It had remained a sacred, calm space that touched each of us. Consider a trip this summer to a place that speaks to your soul, camping in a special place in nature, visiting a retreat that welcomes families, or returning to a spot that had meaning for you as a child.

> *People travel to wonder at the height of the moun-*
> *tains, at the huge waves of the seas, at the long*
> *course of the rivers, at the vast compass of the*
> *ocean, at the circular motion of the stars, and yet*
> *they pass by themselves without wondering.*
>
> —SAINT AUGUSTINE

8

AUGUST

ENCOURAGE FAMILY RESPECT

So often parents ask me, "How do I make my kids respect me and each other?" The answer is to begin respecting your partner and your kids. You might also begin to:

1. Accept and honor the individuality of each family member.
2. Words have power; make yours positive and encouraging.
3. Listen to each other without jumping to early conclusions.
4. Invite people of different cultures and ethnicity into your family life.
5. Respect the meaning and value of all living things—from worms to kings.
6. Share the excitement of each other's dreams and hopes. Support those dreams in appropriate ways.
7. Allow your children to know and respect your role as parents and theirs as children.
8. Do your best to give each child private time away from the rest of the family.
9. Model graciousness and kindness when you interact with others.
10. Look for and respect the divine spirit that links us all.

SOULFUL READING

Summer is the perfect time to dive into good books with your child—uplifting, soulful tales that ignite both of your spirits. Don't think of story time as an obligatory few minutes before your young child goes to sleep, but rather a sweet connection through literature that can inspire you both.

Keep a book handy and read in the hammock, while waiting for the camp carpool, under a tent made of sheets, on a bench at the playground, at the beach, in a cozy reading corner piled with pillows.

Kids of all ages like to be read to, even teenagers! I recently read *To Kill a Mockingbird* with Whitney, and the themes initiated lots of rich discussion. My husband read *Expect Miracles,* by Mary Ellen Angelscribe, to both daughters and their wonder and expectant open attitude were heightened as a result. They saw miracles all around them.

Turn down the volume of your racing thoughts, even if just for fifteen minutes. Snuggle up with your child and one of the soulful books listed in the resource section. You'll find stress melting away as you journey through a good story.

BALANCING TIPS

Reading serves as one of the biggest balancing tools in my life. I can't fall asleep without reading at least a few pages of a book. My bedside table is piled high with books of all kinds, thanks to our wonderful local library. Include reading in your life. You *can* make the time—substitute a good book for the newspaper. Your child will follow your example and seek rest through reading.

⸺☙ Make sure to explore your local library as a family. I have always treated the library as a sacred place, so my kids have that same reverent feeling. We whisper to one another as we discover treasure after treasure in the shelves. We have a designated library bag that carries home these treasures, and we rank our librarians right up there with important people in our lives. The children took part in the library's summer reading program for many years, listing all the books they had read on a designated form. They always looked forward to the ritual of signing up on the first day of summer vacation.

> *One of the things I love the most about summer is that there is time to be read to in the day part of the day.*
>
> —AGE 6

OVERCOMING OBSTACLES

A reporter, interviewing me for a parenting magazine, wanted to know what obstacles block families from creating a sense of spirituality. Not wanting to dwell on the negatives, I tried to refocus her to the natural, everyday opportunities parents have to create a sense of soulfulness within their families. "It's really not hard," I assured her. "Anyone can weave spirituality into their family routine." But she insisted, "What keeps people from getting there?" As I shifted my thinking to the people with whom I have worked, I realized that there are indeed some consistent obstacles to creating a spiritual connectedness in families. See if any of the following feel familiar:

• Lack of time seems to be a consistent deterrent for creating balance. We are moving at a frenzied tempo. Our lives are filled with deadlines, chores, meetings, obligations. Our children's lives are overflowing with lessons, sports practice, rehearsals, appointments, tasks. This habitual pace of constant motion becomes our rhythm. Families have a hard time honoring anything that doesn't have a quantitative result. "If it doesn't get me there faster or isn't on my list of To Do's I don't have time for it." It's important to step out of that mentality and remember we can choose how we spend our time, and it is through our choices that we create a sense of the sacred within our families.

• We can become confused between spirituality and religion. Spirituality involves an awareness of a sacred connection to all creation and a choice to embrace that connection with love. It is the consciousness that relates us directly to God, who is much bigger than any one religion. Spirituality is not the dogma of organized religion, although organized religion provides a great deal to nurture a child's soul. Not something to be taught to a child, spirituality exists already.

• Our own spiritual searching can get in the way of establishing a spiritual connection with our kids. We may question religion because of our past experience. Because we aren't clear about our own beliefs, we are reluctant to begin a dialogue with our children. Don't wait! Take your child's hand and begin a spiritual journey. Explore together rather than avoiding this essential aspect of your child's being.

• A partner's lack of support can hold us back from forging a spiritual path for our family. A mother of three wrote: "When I light a candle in the morning and ask my kids to join hands for a moment of silence my husband just rolls his eyes." And a father of four told me how difficult it was to make time for church on Sundays because his wife wouldn't make the commitment with him. It can be tough to create a spiritual home when our partner doesn't join in our efforts. We can't change people. We can, however, live our own spiritual lives boldly and strive to keep communication open. You are a mirror for your children and show them how spirituality and daily life merge. Mirror it authentically without dimming your light for fear of ridicule. Make an effort to communicate with your partner in the next few days, if you haven't already; discuss ways to merge your beliefs and begin fostering a shared sense of spirituality with your kids.

• We usually respond to children's behavior rather than seeing the whole child. Our children's spiritual natures are reflected by their unbounded creativity, vivid imagination, and joyful, open-ended approach to life. We can mistake this exuberance for hyperactivity, disobedience, or being out of control. Children are beautiful, open spirits housed in human form. Living a spiritual life doesn't imply that they are little gurus who sit with crossed legs and chant all day. Kids wear their spirituality openly, and it flows through the ups and downs of growing up. Begin to look for the spiritual light that glows beneath the antics and listen for the wise knowing beneath the silly prose.

• Cool technology can diminish the worth of humans. It is our role to help kids remain connected to real people, not just E-mail pals, chat room friends, or television characters. We must remember to use technology as a tool rather than an uninvited guest blasting into our homes. Keep the computer in a central place where you can use it together and the television in a spot that takes some effort to reach so that you use it more thoughtfully. Don't allow technology to squelch the less attention-getting but more profound inner spirit that is awaiting your child's discovery.

These are the obstacles that may hinder your spiritual parenting journey. If any one of them feels familiar—explore it in more detail. Becoming aware of our blocks can open the way to greater balance.

LITTLE TOUCHES CREATE LARGE RIPPLES

Think of your home as a living, breathing organism. As you respect and become attentive to your home, the positive effect ripples over into your family. This isn't about creating a magazine layout or making yourself crazy whipping through your house to add meaningful accessories. Rather, adding beauty and meaning, as you are inspired, to the space you call home. It includes honoring your children's artistic visions and ideas and respecting their treasures as cherished additions.

B A L A N C I N G   T I P S

— Fill a shallow dish or basket with small seashells you collect with your kids—scented with oil it becomes a potpourri.

— Larger shells can be used as candleholders or placed along a ledge, shelf, or mantel.

— Displaying photographs that mark important family events can give rooms warmth and grace. Your kids can create funky frames from driftwood, construction paper, poster board. Rather than hanging them, prop them up on the floor, on top of books, or over the kitchen cabinets so you can rotate the collection. Consider investing in a camera for your older children. It's fascinating to view the world from their lens.

— Lighting candles immediately creates a festive feeling. Light lots of them with your kids. Try tiny votive candles on windowsills, fat pillar candles on a pretty plate, floating candles in a cut-glass bowl, scented candles in mismatched holders placed on a round mirror, homemade beeswax candles, outdoor candle pots, lanterns, chunky colored candles in terra-cotta pots painted by kids, tiny tapers held by clay holders—made by tiny hands.

—⌒ Pick up an inexpensive "shoe tray" at your local five-and-ten. Paint it a fun color or even line it with a funky material. Place the tray near your front door and encourage everyone to leave their shoes, along with their worries, at the door.

—⌒ Cleaning is not usually a "fun" thing to do. But if we clean with the intention to make room for positive energy to flow, flow it will. Throw open the windows, even in the winter, and intend for the fresh air to fill your home with new ideas. Think of the stale air and old limiting ideas going right out the windows.

—⌒ Create "interest tables" that are small displays of items of interest to a family member. Perhaps your horse lover could create an equestrian display using horse statues, her horse artwork, the ribbon she won at a show. Maybe she will prop a horse poem on a statue and display a little box with a horse etched on the lid that holds a scrap of paper on which her dream to own a horse is written.

—⌒ Wreaths have wonderful symbolic significance—the circle of life. Add them throughout your home. Kids can fashion wreaths using objects from the earth, such as pine cones, seaweed, greens, cranberries, feathers, seed pods, twigs. Pick up some florist wire and wire cutters and you're in business.

Home is where the house is.

—AGE 5

QUESTIONING SPIRIT

At a certain age children may question or push against spirit, as we've defined it, and begin their own journey toward knowing God. It can come as a jolt when our kids challenge the spiritual ideas we've made such an effort to model, encourage, and experience together.

We want to give our kids the gift of faith along with dental check-ups and good manners. It doesn't always work that way. What we can provide is a spiritual base, a grounding center, a place to begin their journey—remembering that it is *their* journey. "I don't believe in God" from your thirteen year old can punch a panic button you didn't realize you had.

Listen to his worries, challenges, and hopes. Be sensitive to your child's temperament and changes and respectful of his need to be heard—even when he delivers this message in a defiant way. He may be focused on the scientific and quantifiable. Many kids want proof, especially during adolescence. After listening, if appropriate, you can respond to your child by saying, "You're right, it's hard to believe in God as an old man with a long, white beard. That's not the God I sense either. I feel an energy, a God force that I believe is within all of us. We're all connected by this force of good—of God. Is that something that feels right to you?" Listen and listen some more.

We may address the same doubts from our five year old in a loving way. But when our teen questions us in a defensive tone, we panic or feel attacked. We worry that this child will somehow disconnect from all that we have worked so lovingly to keep intact within her. This is when we can shift to a loving heart, and acknowledge her questions with acceptance, realizing that she is branching out on her own, perhaps deeper, relationship with spirit.

Your child's spiritual doubts aren't intended to defy your belief system; they simply are the beginning of a lifelong spiritual growth. Join your child in this quest instead of allowing fear to push you away.

Trust that your child has spiritual roots in place that ground him as his branches stretch and move toward their unique spot in the sky. His questioning allows the branches to twist and grow toward the light. Your challenge is to tune into your changing child's spiritual self periodically. Kid's ideas shift faster than we can catch up. Make the time to meet them where they are today rather than where you *think* they might be.

BALANCING TIPS

—◦ Provide time and support for your child's spiritual exploration. Find a meditation class for kids, begin attending church services more regularly, seek out books with spiritual themes, look for a teen group that is involved in community service, create a DO NOT DISTURB sign for your child's door to signal he is in the midst of private time, practice yoga together, or simply include more conversations about spirituality in your daily routine.

—◦ Share what you believe again and again—in a casual way.

—͡ᵔ Sprinkle some magic around—even if sarcastic comments are made because the enchantment may begin to fade during adolescence.

—͡ᵔ Continue to require appropriate behavior, but find a way to listen to your child through what may be a less-than-delightful attitude.

—͡ᵔ Help kids overcome the attitude that God is waiting to reject them. "If God loves me, why can't I get my locker open?"

> *Our heritage and ideals, our code and standards—*
> *the things we live by and teach our children—are*
> *preserved or diminished by how freely we exchange*
> *ideas and feelings.*
>
> —WALT DISNEY

JUST ANOTHER FAMILY MORNING

I like to spend the soft time between sleep and wakefulness visualizing and praying for the day ahead. It's about the only time I have to settle into that blissful place of complete relaxation. About 5:00 this morning I dreamily began my meditation—our fat kitty snuggled beside me purring with the rhythm of my breath.

All of a sudden the peace was shattered as Comet, our cocker spaniel puppy, tore into the bedroom, leapt on the bed, and chased the hissing cat around the room and down the stairs. 'Round and 'round they went, Comet barking, kitty hissing, nails click-clicking on the hardwood floor. The commotion awakened Elizabeth, who, thinking it was time for school, made her bed, brushed her teeth, and pulled on her favorite pants and sweater.

I tried to settle back into the comfort of my cozy bed, placing my lavender pillow over my eyes for a little extra help in returning to bliss. "Not so fast!" my busy household seemed to shout as Elizabeth pounced in next to me, slithering into my husband's spot—choice pickings when he is traveling.

Cat and dog had stopped their crazed chase by now, and all was a little too quiet downstairs. I stumbled down to investigate, only to discover a yellow puddle soaking into my pale pink living room carpet and a relieved dog wagging his frisky little tail. There's nothing like warm dog tinkle to jolt one out of a morning fog. I blotted and scrubbed, scolded and rinsed. More motion upstairs as Whitney appeared sleepy eyed at the top of the stairs. Out went the dog—on went the carpet spray—back to bed went the mommy, now with a little girl on either side. Ahhhh, I thought, now I can return to that lovely place in my morning consciousness. Deep breathing helped lull me back.

"My head itches, Mama," muttered my long-limbed daughter as she wrapped those limbs around mine. "I hope I don't have head lice. I forgot to tell you but six kids in my class were sent home yesterday with lice, and Becky has it, too." Elizabeth had spent Friday night at Becky's house, sharing a pillow and no doubt nits. This news not only jolted me up once again but jolted my stomach into complete nausea. I turned on every light in the bedroom and began to examine each strand of long, long, long blonde hair—my own head itching with the mere thought of sucking insects in my bed. No evidence of any lice sent us back for a few more minutes of rest. We ignored the dog scratching at the front door, closed our eyes, and arranged ourselves—Elizabeth's hand in mine, Whitney's head on my shoulder.

After a few minutes Elizabeth nudged me and whispered, "Mom, do you see that beautiful angel sitting on the couch? Her name is Marie, and she has the most amazing golden curls. She's here now and she always seems to come when things get a little hectic or when I can't sleep. I feel better now just seeing Marie." I felt better, too. I snuggled my precious daughters even closer. Head lice, dog pee, cat and dog fight, and an angel named Marie—and it's only 7:00 A.M.

BALANCING TIP

Remember that even within the chaotic times there is a spiritual balance waiting to be found. We often just forget to look. Look today. Beneath the mounds of dirty clothing, unopened bills, and dishes in the sink, you might find the guardian spirit of your home. See the brilliant soul beneath your four year old's red tantruming face. Recognize the presence that fills you, guides you, and never deserts you beneath your rattled state of mind.

> *Not everything that can be counted counts, and not everything that counts can be counted.*
>
> —ALBERT EINSTEIN

> *Grown-ups never understand anything for themselves, and it is tiresome for children to be always and forever explaining things to them.*
>
> —ANTOINE DE SAINT-ÉXUPÉRY

9

SEPTEMBER

BACK TO SCHOOL

Children are loading up their new backpacks and heading off to school. It can be a bittersweet transition for parents. We will miss our kids and the easy summer rhythm, but we are ready to embrace more time for ourselves. We want our children to be excited about learning, have supportive friends, look forward to each school day, and be positively challenged. Most of all, we want our child's precious spirit to remain intact.

As my children enter a new grade, I want to jump inside the teacher's skin and give his or her consciousness a knock, knock, knock to let them know that these are sensitive, kind, open girls and to please recognize their grand spirits. I want to pin a note to my daughter's shirt that reads ATTENTION—PRECIOUS CARGO INSIDE. Instead I wrote the following ten Tips for Teachers.

Pass the list along to your child's new teacher. You might include a note that says something like:

> Thank you for committing to teach my child this year. He/She will be spending more time during the week with you than with me. I know you will nourish my son/daughter's mind and wanted to share these ideas on nourishing his/her soul.

You might even deliver a cup of steaming tea or coffee with your note.

TEN WAYS TO CREATE A
NOURISHING CLASSROOM

1. Create a morning ritual to center and unify the children.
2. Take a look at the rhythm of your typical day. Make sure there is flexibility within the structure. Be willing to change course to follow children's interests.
3. Create a class journal. This is a blank book left in a convenient place for anyone to write in. It is a place for even the quietest student to be heard. It could be a fantastic brainstorming device.
4. Have a weekly class meeting. Begin the meetings by asking each person to compliment or thank someone in the group.
5. Bring more nature into the room. Plant seeds or bulbs for each student to tend to. Open the curtains, turn off the overhead lighting, open a window, let the sun shine in.
6. Help children ask of themselves, "What is it I might give," rather than, "What might I get." Encourage students to come up with a class project that allows them to contribute their skills to a cause they feel strongly about.
7. Write a letter a week. Children can write to their heroes, someone in their family, a person they have read about, their favorite author, a pen pal from another country, a child they've been matched with from a higher or lower grade.
8. Acknowledge, respect, and use your intuition or gut feelings. Before beginning your day, pause and go within. Ask quietly, "What do the children need from me today?" Then listen to the answers that come.
9. Ask children to write about or draw their Peaceful Place. This is a place they create in their imaginations and can return to anytime they need a sense of calm.

10. Remember that each day is a new beginning. You can start
     fresh today being just the teacher your class needs. Start fresh
     each day with your students—letting go of old definitions of
     who they are.

B A L A N C I N G   T I P S

—☙ When you send your children off to school, try the following to
help release them to their highest good: "I let go of worry and see my
children surrounded in a bubble of loving care. Their minds are alert
and their bodies are healthy and strong. As they leave for school today, I
trust that they are surrounded by loving angels. My kids reach out with
kindness and are treated kindly by others. Their teachers have patience
and are the perfect match for them. My children's hearts are open, and
they return to me joy-filled, safe, and at peace."

—☙ Establish a tradition for the evening before the first day of
school—eating at a favorite restaurant, one last cookout on the beach,
reviewing summer pictures, organizing new school clothes in the
bureau, a beauty pampering with facial masks and back rubs. Mollie,
mother of five, makes a school bus cake and has a family awards ceremony for everything from the most books read over the summer to the
biggest bug bites.

—☙ Make sure you have at least one reliable backup for your children if they can't contact you. Put that person's phone number in their
school pack or near the phone.

I like a teacher who gives you something to take
home to think about besides homework.

—EDITH ANN (LILY TOMLIN)

TEN WAYS FOR PARENTS TO
HELP TEACHERS DO THEIR JOBS

Many teachers have written to me over the years, frustrated with how unprepared their students are—and they don't mean academically. Chris, a kindergarten teacher, wrote what many teachers have expressed: "I would love it if you could write tips for parents to help us teachers do our increasingly demanding job. Many parents of children I teach have left the job of spiritual, character, and social/emotional education to me. I can't do it all in addition to teaching academic skills. I'm getting burned out and pretty soon won't have the energy left to nourish one child let alone twenty-five."

So here goes:

1. Create a smooth takeoff each day. Give your child a hug before she ventures out the door, look her in the eye and tell her how proud you are of her. Your child's self-confidence and security will help her do well both in school and in life.

2. Prepare for a happy landing at the end of the day. Welcome your child home with a predictable ritual and make yourself available to listen.

3. Fill your child's lunch box with healthy snacks and lunches. Have dinner at a reasonable hour and a healthy breakfast. A well-balanced diet maximizes your child's potential.

4. Include calm, peaceful times in your children's afternoons and evenings. Maintain a schedule that allows them to go to school rested, and if they are sick, have a system in place so they are able to stay home.

5. Remember, it's your children's homework not yours. Create a specific homework space that's clutter-free and quiet. Encourage editing and double-checking, but allow your kids to make mistakes as it's the only way teachers can gauge if they understand the material. It's also how children learn responsibility for the quality of their work.

6. Fill your child's life with a love for learning by showing him your own curiosity, respecting his questions, and encouraging his efforts.

7. Fill your home with books to read, books simply to look at, and books that provide answers to life's many questions. The library is an excellent resource.

8. Be a partner with your child's teacher. When you need to speak to him or her in reference to a specific issue with your child, do it privately, not in front of your child. Make a point to never criticize a teacher in front of your child.

9. Set up a system where routine items are easily located—backpacks, shoes, signed notices. Create a central calendar for upcoming events to avoid the unexpected.

10. Tuck a "love note" in your child's lunch bag to let her know just how special she is. Knowing they are loved makes it easier for children to be kind to others.

ACCEPTING GIFTS

We are easing back into an early bedtime and creating fall order in a summer-filled house. Elizabeth and I went through her clothes and filled three bags with what suddenly didn't fit. She was excited about passing each item along to family friends with four young girls. We rushed over to their home, and Elizabeth created a boutique of sorts to make selecting clothes more fun. Elizabeth's joy in giving matched the four sister's excitement as they donned favorite items. A party was born. As often is the case, our children are our teachers. These dancing, bouncing girls were my models of gracious receivers.

Accepting gifts is often harder than giving them. I know a woman who gives gifts that are thoughtful, exquisite, and exactly what the receiver dreamed of. And yet this same woman shifts her eyes and mumbles an insincere, "Thanks," when a gift is bestowed upon her. She doesn't write thank-you notes or acknowledge receiving gifts in any way.

It's hard for the universe to give us abundance when we've created barriers for acceptance. This woman wonders why she is often unable to meet her financial goals, is in debt, and hasn't had a promotion recently.

Accepting the gifts in our lives graciously opens the way for more blessings to appear. We are a link in the chain of giving and receiving. Let's become gracious receivers and help our children accept gifts with gratitude and joy.

Elizabeth left our impromptu party yesterday with a happy heart and a plate full of luscious brownies. Her closet and bureau look pretty wonderful too—finally they are neat and tidy.

Giving opens the way for receiving.
—FLORENCE SCOVEL SHINN

FOCUS

Having a strong, clear vision creates excitement and a renewed sense of purpose. As we enter a new semester of life—that's what autumn always feels like to me—it's a great time to focus on our visions and goals.

Begin by asking yourself some important questions. If you aren't clear on what's meaningful to you, your life will be full of vague confusion. It's easier to parent from a grounded place when you articulate your convictions.

Make a list of what you believe in—time with family, serenity, making a difference.

I believe in . . .

1.
2.
3.
4.
5.

What about your family? Have you discussed what you as a group believe in? Decisions become easier when kids have an applicable hierarchy of values and beliefs to use as a framework—to look after the earth instead of adding to the problem, choosing to love instead of hate, to forgive instead of holding a grudge, to reach out to someone in need instead of choosing silence.

My family believes in . . .

1.
2.
3.

4.

5.

When we identify our deepest beliefs and guiding principles, it's much easier to prioritize our goals.

> *Clarity of purpose exposes the foundation of the inner heart.*
>
> —UNKNOWN

RAISING CHILDREN IN AN E-MAIL WORLD

I was part of a panel recently that focused on teens and spirituality. A bright fourteen-year-old boy sitting next to me announced that as far as he could see human brains were just "wet computers." This same young man connected with classmates via instant messages but hadn't been to a dance in the three years he'd attended middle school.

Kids long for connection, and technology is fulfilling that desire by allowing them access to worlds beyond their own neighborhoods. But with this vast expansion of opportunity comes a need for balance and consciousness. If our child is exploring nature through vividly graphic Internet sites without running barefoot in the backyard or spying on birds building their nests, there is no balance. When our teenagers connect with cyber pals thousands of miles away but don't take the time to toss a few balls with the kids next door, they don't have the experiential opportunity to know people in all their complexity.

Rather than condemning and fearing the power of today's technology, however, we can accept its potential for good in our family and craft a plan to use it in ways that enhance, rather than shrink, warm human connections.

Here's how to use technology to nurture your child's soul, not just his skills:

BALANCING TIPS

—෴ Examine your own use of technology. Do you rush home from work only to check your E-mail, phone messages, and pager before sitting down to hear about your child's day? One father was devastated to receive this E-mail from his eight-year-old daughter. "Dad, I know how busy you are, but do you think you would have time to read me a story tonight?" He was on his laptop in the family room, she on her computer upstairs in her bedroom.

—෴ Take time to connect as a family. Dazzling technology can diminish the worth of humans. Make your family time count. Come up with specific activities you will take part in together and mark them on the family calendar.

—෴ Find Web sites that enrich your child's life rather than those that encourage spending or show vapid content. Explore these sites together. A couple to check out are playmusic.org, where you can learn about composers and go backstage with a symphony orchestra, and amazing-kids.org, where kids can post their own creative writing.

—෴ Whenever possible, make computer use a social experience: Put the computer in a central place in your home, and put two chairs there to encourage sharing. Get to know what programs interest your child and join him in a simulated city construction or interactive chess game. An added bonus: Older kids are apt to use technology more responsibly when it is out in the open rather than in their bedrooms.

—↬ Learn something new with your kids or share your hobby with the family. Carving out time to come together through a shared activity unites us, parent and child, and grounds us as a family.

—↬ Ask your kids to write a letter a week—longhand. They can write to whomever they choose: family, friends, heroes, someone they read about in the paper. Encourage thank-you notes for gifts but also for everyday kindness. Letter writing is a soulful activity—don't let it disappear.

—↬ Be available to listen to your child's worries and questions. According to a recent national survey by The Henry J. Kaiser Family Foundation, 39 percent of preteens are getting information about their big questions via television or on the Internet. Wouldn't you rather your kids come to you?

—↬ Help your child understand that people control the computer, not the other way around.

—↬ Talk to your kids about what your family believes in when it comes to media. "We only allow programming into our home that treats people respectfully—that goes for Web sites, CDs, video games, and TV shows." Then discuss *why* you feel the way you do, rather than handing out rules and consequences.

—☙ Come up with ways to extend computer interests your kids have into real-world interests. For instance, if your child loves drawing house plans on 3D Home Architect, pick up an inexpensive home plan magazine, buy some graph paper and have your child draw a house design freehand, or call a local architect and ask if you and your child might visit her office for a tour.

—☙ Don't let screen time substitute for lap time with your young child, and don't expect books on CD-ROM to substitute for a loving parent's voice.

SET ASIDE SACRED TIME

I am often asked if being a spiritual parent means taking our children to church or temple each week. We want to do the right thing for our kids and give them all they need to develop into secure, happy, successful, and spiritual beings.

Organized religion, for many, has been the only answer to this need. "I'll take my child to church on Sunday and that part of his development is taken care of." Let's open the definition of sacred time, and rather than limit spirituality to a weekly obligation, become aware of the glorious opportunities during everyday life to celebrate God with our children.

Sacred time can be built into the structure of our days. This might be fifteen minutes of quiet time, gratitudes shared at dinner, a quiet space for reflection in the backyard, a box for children's letters to God, evening rituals before sleep.

Traditional religion provides rituals and ceremonies that are meaningful for many. But spiritual parenting isn't limited to the teachings of Sunday school or Hebrew school. It is the ordinary, everyday existence we lead with our children, the routine and rhythm, the ups and downs. Marnie, mother of a three year old, told me, "Each morning, while the grass is still wet, no matter how rushed, we go for a brisk walk together. At the end of the day, we curl up together and read or just tell a story from our past."

We nourish our children's spirituality and give them assurance in the face of life's difficulties when we help them understand they have instant access to a greater loving power at all times, then show them how to go within for this guidance. It's not our parental obligation to force beliefs upon our kids but our joy to keep their natural spirit alive and growing. It can be a delight to share our own spiritual quest with our family and journey together.

BALANCING TIPS

—◌ Select a specific time as your family's sacred time to be with God. If you don't attend a religious ceremony, you could spend time in the woods writing in your journals, or if your child is too young to write, she might draw her visions and ideas. Ask your children to create a ceremony at home, complete with prayers they have written and songs they have selected.

—◌ Think of your family as a sacred congregation. Exploring things together builds a common appreciation of life. Listen to various kinds of music, open your eyes to the world around you, collect rocks from your hikes, plant broccoli instead of carrots, attend the local artisan fair and agree on a favorite piece of pottery.

⟶ Listening nourishes our spirits. There is listening to one another, through conversation, attending to words not spoken, eavesdropping, and then there is inner listening. Giving our children the gift of appreciating silent listening as a response to life and access to spirit is extraordinary. How do we wrap up this sacred bundle and lay it at the feet of our son or daughter? First of all, we must work against our natural inclination to provide our kids with constant stimulus to keep them from becoming bored or help them move up the learning curve. The simple act of creating quiet time at home can be a relief for kids. Through the silence, and our example, they will find their way to inside listening and the availability of spirit that calms, blesses, consoles, and calls them in for more.

⟶ Spirituality is the consciousness that relates us directly to God, or whatever we name as the source of our being. That consciousness can be activated when we are making a mud pie, singing our gratitudes, observing a spider web, or are deep in meditation. When we are sensitive to our child's sense of time—we all know how different it can be from that of adults'—we enable them to remain connected with what might be a sacred moment. Rather than explaining how the spider spun her web, we can enter into the magic of the moment and observe the intricate design with our toddler. Setting aside sacred time means more than just manipulating our calendar. It is an awareness of and an authentic response to life's simple, always available gifts.

⟶ Taking our children's questions seriously helps foster their spiritual development. Rather than giving them pat answers, we might ponder life's mysteries along with them. Each question asked can become a sacred exchange, even if it's in the car on the way to school and work, with breakfast sandwich in hand and traffic up ahead.

> *Balancing career and home relationships is an almost impossible daily routine task. Only through spiritual parenting can this reach any semblance of happening. Only through making everything I do a living prayer, is this possible for me.*
>
> —MOTHER OF FOUR

> *Whether we call it a higher power, consciousness, or the universe, there is an extraordinary source of energy and intelligence to tap into.*
>
> —AUTHOR UNKNOWN

BEDROOMS WHERE DREAMS ARE SPUN

Kids need an oasis from the "world out there" to find their balance and return to their center. Even if they share a room, your children can have a bedroom that facilitates rest, recharging, daydreaming, creativity, and quiet time. It doesn't take a decorator to create a soulful bedroom. Try one of the following:

• Allow your child's room to be a safe base for soulful exploration. Give him a choice in color, fabric, furniture. Allow her to decorate the door with silver paint, if she so desires, or collage the closet with images she loves cut from magazines.

• Make sure your child can reach important things. If not, invest in a sturdy stepping stool.

• If your kids share a room, ensure that each has privacy—bookcases or rice paper panels to divide the space is one solution.

• Create a bed suitable for reading with a safe, well-placed lamp and comfortable reading pillows. The association with books and reading will be a good one. A nine year old told me, "I like to read in bed because it is my safe, cozy place. I know I won't be disturbed and I feel all tucked in and nice."

• Hang sheets from the ceiling on all four sides of your child's bed if she wants a cozy, private, snug nest. Purchase curtain rods from the hardware store that screw into the ceiling. Sew tabs on the sheets and hang them up for a low cost, royal canopy bed. An eleven year old has the perfect retreat from a world that's spinning out of control. "I have drawn pictures of my dream bed since I was four years old. I finally have it. I wanted a bed with curtains all around it so I could close them and no one would see me. Now I have yellow curtains hanging on all sides of my bed and my dog and I snuggle in for the night. I look forward to that cozy place all day."

• Use natural fabrics in bedrooms. Synthetic materials used in nightclothes, sheets, or duvet covers are hot and cause lots of static shocks.

• Buy or make some scented eye pillows for every bed in the house. Silk material is the most luxurious, filled with dried lavender and dried lentils or rice.

• Don't get rid of the rocking chair when your child has outgrown the nursery. Many a child has needed a gentle rocking, "Just like when I was a baby."

• Invest in a storage system for the closet or create your own out of baskets and bins. Kids have a better chance at creating order when everything has a place.

And what about your bedroom? So many parents have told me th. a serene and orderly bedroom was pivotal for creating balance. After all, it's the first and last space you see each day. A mother of three was experiencing insomnia. She greeted each morning worn out, only to lie awake again each evening. I suggested she move her desk out of the bedroom; it was piled with work she brought home from the office. She did so and she also established a few destressing evening rituals after the children were in bed, such as a hot bath, soothing music, candlelight, and journal writing. That was just the tonic she needed to fall asleep.

BALANCING TIPS

—҈ Soft lighting, sheets in soothing shades, gentle artwork all contribute to the sense of ease in your bedroom.

—҈ Invest in a good mattress and comfy pillows. Since we spend one-third of our lifetimes in bed, shouldn't it be as comfortable as possible?

—҈ Lavender placed near the bed does a great job of inducing sleep. You can buy dried lavender at most health food stores or drop lavender oil on a cotton ball and tuck it behind your pillow.

)UR CONNECTION TO SPIRIT

:re told that your life was a sacred prayer your child took as the ~~~ for a spiritual existence? When we acknowledge ourselves first and foremost as spiritual beings, we can't help but shift our parenting energy into a higher place. Exploring our own sacred selves enhances our connection with our kids.

As spiritual parents we want to ignite, enhance, and empower the divine light our children come to us with. We can't do that, however, without also recognizing our own magnificent and powerful light. When we attend to our own spirits, everyone in our family benefits.

Laurie lives with her husband, two sons, two stepdaughters, and her elderly mother. She maintains, "The demeanor of our house revolves around my inner stress level. When I'm stressed, everyone's stressed. I'm the gauge, so it's important for me to be balanced. My family knows I need at least fifteen minutes of quiet time alone in my bedroom. When the door is shut, that's their signal that Mom is replenishing her patience. I listen to music, knit, or just close my eyes and feel the presence of spirit."

One mother sings as a way to revitalize her soul and has introduced her children to music, hoping they will find it as rich a spiritual tool as she has. A single father of four lets his spirit soar on his bike. "I am much happier and more connected to spirit when I exercise, so I pass up lunches out so I can ride my bike. It clears my head and gets me outdoors. I want the time after work to be with my kids so lunchtime riding is the perfect solution."

Marianna, mother of a special needs child, finds that savoring the day rather than marching through it balances her many roles. "I slow down and see the beauty the day holds. I try to stay out of my inner life fog, seeking instead clarity of vision. This makes a cloudy day beautiful.

I try to harmonize my thoughts and emotions with the work of my hands, which takes my focused, fully concentrated attention. This is my spiritual inner life harmonizing with the daily work I must do."

As you create space to nourish your spiritual life, whether through organized religion, a connection with nature, meditation, yoga, music, or being with friends, you invite the angel of serenity to descend upon you. You will begin to notice more and more grace mysteriously moving you forward and a renewed reserve of strength.

BALANCING TIPS

—❧ Find a basket or special box and fill it with items that inspire you—a blank journal, uplifting books, a candle, photos that touch your heart. Then give yourself fifteen minutes each day to be with these soulful tools. I've been able to grab time in the early morning before my children awaken. Reading a contemplative thought or jotting down ideas in my journal are rituals that launch me into my day.

—❧ Make the early morning hours your connection time. Brew up some tea or coffee and indulge yourself in the quiet, the warm liquid, the possibilities that lie ahead. Wendy says, "My day begins with a cup of coffee in bed and then about fifteen minutes of meditation. My job is busy and my two young children need me in the morning. This is *my* time with coffee and quiet."

—❧ Choose to be around positive people who feed you rather than dim your energy.

—☞   Listen to inspirational books on tape when you are commuting to work or exercising. It can be a shot of positive energy rather than a radio's assault of depressing news and monotonous commercials.

—☞   Recognize the challenges you face as hidden opportunities to grow. Rather than become attached to problems, intend to release them and begin to visualize how you would like your life to unfold—sans difficulty.

—☞   Allow yourself to think and dream in unlimited ways. We do this for our children, seeing the vision of who they might become and the great things they will accomplish. Let's expand the vision we hold for ourselves.

> *The greatest discoveries will be along spiritual lines. This is the field where miracles are going to happen. Spiritual power is the greatest underdeveloped power and has the greatest future.*
>
> —THOMAS EDISON

> *I leave spiritual reading in the bathroom. I'm bound to be there alone for a few minutes a few times a day.*
>
> —MOTHER OF THREE

Resources

PART THREE: SUMMER

Adult Books

Benson, John. *Transformative Getaways*. New York: Henry Holt, 1996. A directory of fantastic journeys.

Gawain, Shakti. *Creative Visualization*. San Rafael, CA: New World Library, 1983. One of the clearest guides ever written on how to create the life of your dreams.

Lederman, Ellen. *Vacations That Can Change Your Life*. New York: Source-books, Inc., 1996. A little dated, but still full of ideas and resources for further exploration.

Richardson, Cheryl. *Take Time for Your Life*. New York: Broadway Books, 1999. Cheryl lays out a clear plan for taking charge of the details of your life.

Roman, Sanaya. *Living with Joy*. Tiburon, CA: H. J.Kramer, 1986. My tattered copy is a continued source of inspiration.

Kids

Bea, Holly. *Where Does God Live?* Tiburon, CA: Starseed Press, 1997. A sweet book that asks the question many kids wonder about.

Curtis, Chara. *All I See Is Part of Me*. Bellevue, WA: Illumination Arts, 1994. My favorite line from this wise book is: "Your body is just a little part of the light that shines within your heart."

Loomans, Diane. *The Lovables in the Kingdom of Self-Esteem.* Tiburon, CA:
H. J. Kramer, 1991. A warm, richly illustrated picture book, with affir-
mative words that help kids feel great about themselves. Tanya Turtle,
for instance, demonstrates how she finds peace within.

Millman, Dan. *Secret of the Peaceful Warrior.* Tiburon, CA: H. J. Kramer,
1991. There aren't enough books like this that model ways to show
courage and face fears.

Sasso, Sandy Eisenberg. *God's Paintbrush.* Woodstock, VT: Jewish Lights
Press, 1993. I love this book's way of helping children find God in their
everyday lives.

Older Kids

Berger, Barbara. *Gwinna.* New York: Philomel Books, 1990. This enchanting
story weaves nature with growing up and letting go with loving deeply.
My daughter calls this her "favorite book of life" and has read and
reread it from ages six to ten.

L'Engle, Madeline L'Engle. *A Wrinkle In Time.* New York: Yearling Books,
1973. Reread this fantastic journey with your child.

Rylant, Cynthia. *The Van Gogh Cafe.* New York: Harcourt Brace, 1995. My
family's all-time favorite book. We must have given away a hundred
copies of Rylant's marvelous story about an enchanted cafe and those
who pass through the doors.

———. *The Islander.* New York: D. K. Publishing, 1998. Another magical
book by one of my favorite authors. This one is about a boy's encounter
with a mermaid and a special key that turns his life around.

White, E. B., *Charlotte's Web.* New York: Harper Collins, 1999. Don't forget
this classic book about friendship, miracles, life and death. The
exchange between Fern's parents in chapter 8 is spoken directly to all

parents: "I worry about Fern," she said. "Did you hear the way she rambled on about the animals, pretending that they talked?" Mr. Arable chuckled. "Maybe they do talk. I've sometimes wondered. At any rate, don't worry about Fern—she's just got a lively imagination. Kids think they hear all sorts of things." "Just the same, I do worry about her," replied Mrs. Arable. "I don't think it's normal. You know perfectly well animals don't talk." Mr. Arable grinned. "Maybe our ears aren't as sharp as Fern's," he said.

Wyatt, Isabel. *The Seven-Year-Old Wonder Book*. Edinburgh: Floris Books, 1997. This is the gift I give every child I know turning seven. It's kind of a mystical, mythical guide for the journey of the seventh year. Seven is a pivotal age, it seems, in a child's spiritual development.

Movies

October Sky. A wonderful story about overcoming the odds and going for a dream.

The Long Walk Home. A moving account of the busing protest. Shows a woman standing up for what she believes in—risking family and friends to do what's right.

Some other movies to watch with your children:

The Secret of Roan Irish.
The Miracle Worker.
Our Town.
Andre.
Contact.
The African Queen.

Yentl.

Little Buddha.

Music of the Heart.

Yo u n ğ e r   K i d s

The Sound of Music
My Fair Lady
National Velvet

We b   S i t e s

www.cherylrichardson.com. The companion site to Cheryl's coaching
   books. Sign up for her weekly newsletter.
www.burtsbees.com. Burt's Bees has fantastic, earth-friendly products for
   the whole family. I adore their apricot baby oil dropped in an evening
   bath.

For y o u r t r a v e l e x c u r s i o n s t r y :

Park Locator by L.L. Bean . . . www.llbean.com/parksearch.
Best Scenic Drives . . . www.byways.org.
Wacky Side Trips . . . www.roadsideamerica.com.
Best Greasy Spoon . . . www.astro.princeton.edu/~goldberg/.

D i r e c t i o n s

www.mapsonus.com.
www.mapquest.com.
www.mapblast.com.

www.specialtytravel.com. Gives information about vacations and tour operators.

Web Sites

www. omega-inst.org
    Omega Institute (family program)
    260 Lake Drive
    Rhinebeck, NY 12572-3212
    Check out Omega's wonderful seminars and speakers.

www.kripalu.org
    Kripalu Center for Yoga and Health (children's programs)
    P.O. Box 793
    Lenox, MA 01240
    I've been visiting Kripaula with my daughter for years and there's something special about its setting.

www.unityworldhq.org/dailyword.htm
    Daily Word on line is another way to begin the day.

www.infed.org/biblio/holisticeducation.htm
    Holistic Education Web site offers a depth of reading on how to create a healthier life.

Magazines

Creative Thought Magazine. CreativeThought@rsintl.org. 800-662-1348. Subscribe to this monthly magazine full of daily inspirations.

PART FOUR

FALL

School is back in session and the pace picks up. You need a way to manage your family's schedule rather than allowing it to manage you. In the next few months, you will identify the energy vampires that suck your precious life verve, leaving you weak and wobbly in their wake. Fall is the perfect time to kick up the gratitude response—it will color your children's view of the world. Rather than asking, "What is it I might get?" they will begin to wonder, "What is it I might give?"

Are you long on holiday spirit but short on time? You will find Balancing Tips ahead that will keep you centered during the busy holiday season, along with simple ways to craft holidays with meaning rather than numbly shopping your way through December. ⟞

10

OCTOBER

ACCESS OVERLOAD

This short quiz isn't meant to make you feel guilty about your parenting choices. It's a simple tool to help you examine your child's current schedule. Take it when you have some time to reflect on the structure and rhythm of your child's activities and obligations. It will give you insight into ways to create a more balanced life for your child and your child's chauffeur.

T F

☐ ☐ My child has an after-school activity every day of the week.

☐ ☐ There is no time during the week for my child to get together and play with friends.

☐ ☐ My child has resisted taking a class or signing up for a sport, but I insist.

☐ ☐ There is usually no time during the weekends for our family to reconnect and spend time together.

☐ ☐ We often wake up Monday morning feeling tired.

☐ ☐ If my child isn't signed up for classes or involved in sports, I worry he will lag behind his peers.

☐ ☐ We rarely eat dinner together.

☐ ☐ Bedtime is later than I'd like because homework isn't started until after dinner.

☐ ☐ I don't think my child gets enough enrichment in school so I'm determined she will get it outside of school.

☐ ☐ It's never too soon to begin thinking about college admissions and how my kid will stand out.

Tally up your True and False responses and take a look at your score.

8–10 True: Slow it down. Cut out at least one activity per week. Your child only has one chance to be a kid. Allow him that gift.

4–7 True: Remember, the importance of family time as well as living in the present moment. What action might you take this week to ease up on your busy schedule?

1–3 True: You're aware that children need open-ended free time and you're making an effort. Great job.

MANAGING YOUR CHILD'S SCHEDULE

The common refrain these days seems to be, "Whew . . . life is a whirl. We are *so* busy." It's almost a badge of achievement for some parents to breathlessly describe their "on the run" lives—as if they're giving their child a leg up by being in two sports, a play, music practice, scouts, art lessons, a few clubs, and a little tutoring on the side. Describing their busy schedules seems to validate parents' efforts and suggest they're giving their children stellar advantages. Putting their infant on the wait list for toddler French class, tutoring their preschooler for private kindergarten entrance exams, or phoning their middle schooler's soccer coach demanding more play time assures them they are on top of this project called "parenting."

We are busy parents micromanaging busy kids. We love our children and want to provide everything we can to see them enriched, empowered, and successful. In the midst of all this busyness, however, kids are starving for their parents' attention. What their souls crave much more than another lesson is the loving presence of an adult who listens and cares deeply. They need less pressure to perform and more open-ended time to ponder. Rather than being a project their parents strategically plan, with achievements measured on a corporatelike timeline, kids yearn for a relationship with their mom and dad.

A University of Michigan social research study showed that school-age youngsters have only 30 percent of their day as "free" time to use as they wish. The other 70 percent is packed with classes, part-time jobs after school, homework, and extracurricular activities, like sports.

Just because our own lives might be frenetic with work, family, and the endless tasks of daily life doesn't mean we should program our kids into that rhythm. When we find the balance between offering our children opportunities and running them ragged, our own pace inevitably winds down. When we create a manageable schedule for our kids, we eliminate some of the exhaustion and stress that is consuming far too many of them. Enriching activities do help children learn and grow as their curiosity and interests are fed. But too much of a good thing can hurt.

Our culture doesn't honor the value of free time, but we must. Kids aren't comfortable with quiet as they grow older because they aren't used to it. It's of critical importance to create space in our young children's days for unstructured, open-ended, quiet time. One sixth grader, armed with her Palm Pilot and twenty-pound backpack, declined my daughter's invitation to "hang out at our house" because there wasn't a spot for the next two weeks on her schedule.

How might you begin to claim a slower pace for your family? My friend Robert Gerzon, author of *Finding Serenity in the Age of Anxiety,* is a wonderful model. He says, "My wife and I 'vaccinate' our children against society's time sickness by entering the paradise of the present moment with our children every day. When we play with our children we let them teach us how to leave behind clock time and play in the eternal now."

Perhaps you might find a group of like-minded friends and "Just say *no*" to the seductive lure of overscheduling kids. I know it's easier said than done. I'm still searching for that balance and struggling to find support for my choices.

I grew up in a small town where the only classes available were an odd version of ballet held in the rec room basement of an aging showgirl's split-level house or log rolling with special cleated shoes in frigid Lake Michigan. I played dress-up instead. When my first child was old enough to enroll, I drooled at the possible classes for her—everything from Irish step dancing to yoga for toddlers to Mommy and Me music. When I tuned into my child, I realized what her spirit needed was simple, sweet, playtime. I still have to restrain myself. Just recently I excitedly told my horse-loving daughter that she was about ready to go to shows. "I don't want to compete, Mom," she said. "I just take riding lessons to challenge myself and because I love the horses."

It takes lots of time and enormous energy to allow your child to be a child. I would contend even more energy and imagination than simply organizing a mad schedule of classes. It's easy, albeit exhausting, to "do." It's much harder, but ultimately more nourishing, just to "be." It's more comfortable for some of us to control our kids by providing structured classes than to follow their lead and get down on the floor to play.

Many of us struggle with the balance between gently nudging our children to try things and pushing them too far. Amy, a mother of two, told me of her dilemma with her seven-year-old daughter. "Sarah loves to be alone and to play elaborate imagination games. She cries a lot about having to do too much that takes her away from her room and her 'things.' But do I trust that she is *really* wanting this or just being lazy and manipulative?"

Children's individual temperaments need to be taken into account. Look at your own children to determine the activity level that keeps them on an even keel. Some kids need the energy a group provides and thrive on stimulation, while others are sourced and refueled by curling up on their bed stroking their kitty. Observe your children, listen to them, and follow your own intuition.

Next time you are visiting with someone who makes you feel completely inadequate as a parent because you're not signing your kid up for space camp, gifted enrichment, tap class, soccer, and violin, pause and remind yourself that you are signing your child up for mindfulness, serenity, a closer connection to spirit, free exploration of the junk drawer, and a deeper connection with you. Tell them the lovely African proverb, "No one shows a child the sky," then turn on Simon and Garfunkel's tune "Slow down, you move too fast" and dance around the kitchen with your relaxed kids.

Here are some ideas to help you move off the fast track and onto the family lane.

BALANCING TIPS

—๛ Create a "no-technology time" in your house and turn off the computers, DVDs, Gameboys, TVs, phones, beepers, Playstations, fax machines, and Walkmans. How great for your kids to "get bored"—

that's where creativity flows in, that's when their inner voice can finally be heard. One family banned electronic devices for the summer and their twelve year old took up whittling. He says, "I hated it at first when my parents gave us their 'no electronics' vote. I missed MTV and all the great video games my brothers and I played. But by August it was pretty cool to see the birds I had carved. I liked the thinking time, too."

—☌ Designate one night a week as Family Night. Rent a movie, pop some popcorn, light a fire, and just be together.

—☌ Establish "Quiet Time" for fifteen minutes a day. Use a timer for your young child.

—☌ Schedule a lesson for every second week rather than weekly. Give your child the free day as playtime.

—☌ Make sure the weekends are a time to rest, daydream, and recharge for the week ahead.

> *I had just started a new school with lots of home-work and had play practice three afternoons a week until dinner. I felt stressed out and pressured that I had to do my homework and learn my lines and make new friends. My mom got worried because I lost ten pounds in one month. I'm not doing any-thing after school now.*
>
> —AGE 9

The secret of life is balance, and the absence of balance is life's destruction.

—HAZRAT INAYAT KHAU

THE GIFT OF GRATITUDE

I received an E-mail from a friend this afternoon with the following question: "What's the best thing that's happened to you today?" I stopped everything I was doing and jotted down my first responses:

- Glorious fall colors right outside my office window—swirling, dancing, golden red leaves.
- A sun-soaked lunch with my nine year old and her new friend.
- Discovering one last piece of scrumptious chocolate cake tucked away in the cupboard, then sitting down with a big glass of milk and loving every bite.

Everything looked a little brighter after this quick little gratitude scan. Try it yourself. Call a friend or send an E-mail to your spouse asking this simple question. When your kids come home at the end of the day greet them with, "Hey, tell me the two best things that happened today before I can count to ten." Or, before bed, suggest your child think of all the good things from the day. He can describe them to you or just call them to mind. What a great way to drift into dreamland.

One of my favorite sayings is, "For that which you are thankful you will never be denied." I wish I knew who said it so I might give that wise soul credit. In the meantime, I've used it enough for squatter's rights.

BALANCING TIP

⌐ Write, on small pieces of paper, several things your family is thankful for. Put these slips into a jar or box and read one when you need a dose of balance. It can keep things in perspective as life spins around you.

Gratitude is heaven itself.

—WILLIAM BLAKE

A PAIN IN THE NECK

There are spots all over my body that hold on to the ordinary tensions of living a family life. The ache in my shoulder holds the unresolved error on my daughter's last semester report card and the teacher who forgets to return calls. A knot in my neck is from juggling pickup time at school today with a radio interview and vet appointment for the cat. My aching jaw is the container for the proposal on my desk rather than in the mail, a stack of unopened letters, and the inspection sticker on my car, which a very nice police officer informed me is six months outdated.

Sometimes I hold my breath, unintentionally, when my mind is racing, which leads to a whopping headache. Balance is shot when a migraine is working its way to the surface. So I've created habits to remind me to breathe, yoga poses to let those sore spots release their clutch, and notepads in the car, on my desk, next to my bed, and near the kitchen phone. When the "to do's" try to slither into my body and take a nasty hold, I take a deep breath and begin another list or take a hot bath or spill out my woes to my patient husband or an understanding friend. When that doesn't work, I pick up the phone and schedule a massage, albeit reluctantly because I, like many women, feel guilty for taking the time and spending the money for something that feels so indulgent.

What strategies help you keep it all together? Are you even aware when the tension is creeping into your body? Do you lose your temper with your kids, rage at yourself for being inadequate, hurl a nasty comment your spouse's way, develop a nasty itch on your hands, throw out your back, eat a few candy bars?

As we juggle our many roles, let's make sure we have lifelines in place. Cheryl, a sales consultant and mother of twin toddlers, told me that she takes care of everyone else's needs until about Thursday, when she goes on an emotional strike and allows herself to say, "No, not now, I'm taking a walk or reading a book or not making a real dinner."

Do a scan, right now, of your body. Where are you holding tension? What is stiff or achy or downright in pain? Ask yourself what that spot is gripping so tightly. Now take a deep breath, write down what steps you can take to handle the issue, and throw out the gooey cookie you're about to gobble down as a distraction from what feels so out of your control.

Karen is a single mom and a busy project manager whose life had to change to deal with stress that lodged in her stomach. She was home with tummy pains for days on end scrambling for help with her son and coverage in the office. "I finally moved to part-time work, have cut back on almost all my volunteer commitments, and grocery shop once a week. I have a weekly menu and a homemade shopping list, organized by aisle, on the fridge so I just check the item when we run out. I've applied budgeting techniques to my life, which has greatly reduced my stress level and allowed me to live on a smaller income. I exercise during my lunch hour at least twice a week; and finally, with all these changes, I'm not in pain and my son and I are both much happier."

Give yourself permission to use balancing techniques and tools that have helped in the past. If you're a better parent after exercising, then don't cancel the dance class for a dentist appointment. If you are more efficient at work when you leave a neat and tidy household, then consider hiring a cleaning person or schedule a family cleanup last thing each evening.

Take control of the details of your life so they don't lodge themselves in your beautiful vibrant body. And if you feel too overwhelmed to hear that, then think of managing your stress so you might give your child the gift of a healthy, balanced, tension-free parent.

B A L A N C I N G   T I P

We all become overwhelmed by the ordinary, never-ending tasks that fill our lives as parents. Make a list of all the things you "should" do in the next few weeks. Take some time and dump it all on paper. Now don't you feel a bit lighter? Better yet, can you begin to laugh at the impossibility of ever getting it all done? Phone a friend and compare lists. Ludicrous what we think must happen before we can rest. I'm exhausted just thinking of the list I have to make.

The happiest people I know are the ones who have learned how to hold everything loosely and have given the worrisome, stress-filled, fearful details of their lives into God's keeping.

—CHARLES R. SWINDOLL

HANG ON TO YOUR DREAMS

Don't discard your own hopes and dreams as merely wishful thinking. Honor them as messages from your soul about your life's plan and what you came here to do. Anything is possible. That is what you want your child to believe and what you can embrace for you both. Your vision of the future will become a road map for creating the life you want. Do you have the map clearly drawn? Show your child a parent who embraces his or her dreams and take steps to create them.

Close your eyes and picture yourself in one year. Are you closer to your dream? How about ten years from now? Really paint the picture clearly. See yourself enjoying your new life and celebrating goals reached. Feel what it's like to have your dream come true. Remember that the life you are living now was your dream five years ago.

Ask yourself if there is enough time for fun in your life. Most of us get to work on time, keep our homes relatively clean, care for our kids, and even get the car in for its scheduled service visits. But what we really enjoy doing, playing tennis, hiking, building model airplanes, writing poetry, may never get done. Part of recapturing our dreams is articulating what we would like to experience in our allotted amount of time on earth.

Get out a piece of paper right now or open your journal and write down fifty things you want to do before you die. Let yourself have a blast with this—don't stop at No. 18. Do you want to soar over New Mexico in a hot air balloon, travel to Tibet, have a part in a movie, write a children's book, attend the Olympics, adopt a child? Go ahead, list your heart's desires without editing. Somehow, compiling our future dreams sets in motion serendipitous events that make things happen. I recently spoke with a woman who said she had made just such a list when she was an eight year old living in less than splendid conditions in Virginia. She is now well past sixty and says that almost every one of those fifty goals has come true. She even shook the hand of the president of the United States, No. 33 on her list.

Ask your kids to create their dream list. Buy them poster board in wonderful colors or simply type the list as they dictate it. Remind them no dream is too fantastic.

> *Dream lofty dreams and as you dream, so you shall become. Your vision is the promise of what you shall one day be; your ideal is the prophecy of what you shall at last unveil.*
>
> —JAMES LANE ALLEN

WHEN OUR KIDS HURT

When our children are little and another child hurts them, we step in and resolve the situation. A toddler pushes our toddler and we put our face down on their level and speak a firm, "No, that isn't nice behavior." As they grow older, however, we can't step in and make everything okay.

The past week has been a painful one for my daughter as her best friend has chosen a replacement. I can't shout, "No," or put my face in front of hers and demand she act more kindly and stop using hurtful words. I want to pick up the phone and request that someone, the child's mother, a teacher, make this right. I want to turn back the clock and have this girl we have known so long take back her exclusionary words and hurtful actions. I want to wrap my sweet, vulnerable daughter's heart in pink cotton to pad it from pain.

Instead, I offer myself; my open arms to hold her, my stories of childhood friend problems, my assurance that she's always supported by her strong foundation of spirit. We affirm together for a positive resolution, we discuss strategies for making new friendships, and we come up with a way she can express her hurt directly to her friend. I remind her that no person or circumstance has the power to keep the joy that God has prepared for her. But there is still a part of me that wants to trip this "ex–best friend" as she skips merrily to school, arm in arm with her new best pal.

Now is the time I can help Elizabeth unpack her spiritual toolbox and move through the pain of today. I can provide a home that supports, grounds, and refuels her as she returns bashed and bruised from the world out there.

I ache for my daughter's pain, her salty evening tears, and her disappointment. Her older sister reminds me that it's important for Elizabeth to work this out on her own as she's going to need lots of practice before, shudder, sixth grade, where this sort of thing happens every day. The tools, strategies, and support we give our children for what appear minor hurts will help them handle the inevitable problems of growing up.

B A L A N C I N G   T I P S

⟶ Create a safe place to listen without probing. Think of yourself as an available, receptive presence.

⟶ Ascertain if there is an appropriate action for you to take, if the situation is dangerous in any way. As much as we want to jump in and fix things, usually it's our child's lesson and we should watchfully step

back. Follow your intuition rather than your racing mind, which wants
to flatten the offending kid's bike tires.

—֍ Create a calm and predictable routine at home. Life may be
topsy-turvy at school, but your child can count on order at home.

—֍ Find someone to support you as you support your child. Dive
into your own spiritual practice for guidance.

—֍ Maybe a day off from school is in order. Grown-ups are entitled
to mental health days, why not kids?

—֍ If appropriate (i.e., no action on your child's part is necessary),
help him or her to let go and let God. Come up with specific strategies
to release the struggle, particularly at bedtime.

> *Our goal, while on this earth, is to transcend our
> illusions and discover the innate power of our
> spirit.*
>
> —CAROLINE MYSS

ENERGY VAMPIRES

Who or what is zapping your energy? Is there a person in your life who is
a constant source of negativity? Does the stain on the living room carpet
or the broken doorbell gnaw away at your peace? Does the smell of the litter box send you over the edge? Are you living with tension about debt?
Barbara is the mother of two and manages a small clothing bou-

tique. Her husband is on the road two weeks a month, leaving her to keep family life orbiting and her own career going. Always exhausted, Barbara treats herself to manicures, facials, and special cups of coffee. Her life seems to be about taking care of others so this is her way to care for herself. When her husband sees the monthly bills, he's irritated at the charges for Barbara's "frivolous treats." But are they?

When Barbara took a look at the energy vampires in her life, she realized what she needed to shift in her schedule in order to create more harmony for herself and her children. Pampering herself was fine, but it was a Band-Aid. Barbara needed to ask for help from others, disengage from coworkers' gossip and petty dramas, create a rhythm to her days, add more order to her home, and find a way to reconnect with her husband. Identifying the areas of her life that were out of balance was the first step in stopping the leaks.

When we start to eliminate the energy drains, we have more enthusiasm, joy, and a greater capacity to manifest what we want in life. Our children have more of us when we aren't being "rubbed the wrong way."

Carla's nine-year-old son helped her identify a big energy vampire in her life. She felt unsettled and edgy every time she prepared to host a volunteer-related function in her home—a church meeting, school event, or planning session. She resented the intrusion the meetings caused in her busy life yet continued to offer her home. When her son, sensing her frustration, asked, "Mommy, why are you having the meeting here when it makes you so crabby?" she finally released that particular energy vampire by no longer offering her house.

Be loving but firm with the energy vampires who also happen to be family members. Take care of yourself and your own life and set clear boundaries. It's okay to say, "No."

Once you are aware of what drags you down, set about making a plan to correct it. You and your family will be better because of it.

BALANCING TIP

Answer the following questions to begin the quest of balancing your life.

1. What's the biggest challenge I face on a daily basis?
2. Who are the energy vampires in my life?
3. How can I free myself from their negativity without being hurtful or unkind?
4. What depletes my energy at work?
5. How might I eliminate these energy drains at work or restructure my day to better handle those that won't go away?
6. What are the energy vampires at home?
7. What one drain can I eliminate or handle differently this week?

Believe me when I say, stay away from the energy vampires. They take and they take and they take— they leave you weak and wobbly in their wake.

—FROM CHRISTINE LAVIN'S SONG "ENERGY VAMPIRES"

Releasing people, habits, activities, and things that were once valuable, but now only serve as dead weights, roadblocks, or as sources of trouble, is a necessary part of every successful person's life.

—TERRY COLE-WHITTAKER

11

NOVEMBER

TRUE THANKSGIVINGS

Thanksgiving is an ideal time to talk to your kids about being truly grateful. It's a natural holiday for creating unique family traditions. Ask your kids to write what they are thankful for on a yearly Thanksgiving poster, from passing a spelling test to sharing life with a beloved Black Lab. Decorate it with festive fall colors, photos, and drawings of their gratitudes. Hang this cornucopia of words and images on the fridge right along with the grocery list for cranberry sauce and potatoes. Haul it out each Thanksgiving to add new appreciations. Remember that Thanksgiving isn't the only time to show gratitude. Here are some year-round ideas for extending this most beautiful of holidays.

Ten Ways to Show Gratitude as a Family!

1. Thank your partner for everyday thoughtfulness—in front of your kids.
2. Change gears and rethink what might otherwise be a complaint. Rather than becoming furious about the sports equipment lying around, think of how grateful you are that your kids are healthy and able to play sports. Then come up with a new family plan for creating order. Help your children practice giving thanks rather than complaining.

3. Begin family dinners by thanking someone at the table for a special kindness they have shown you.

4. Start your children on the wonderful habit of looking the person they are thanking right in the eye.

5. Frequently remind your kids how grateful you are that they were born.

6. Thank-you notes never go out of style. Even the youngest child can draw a picture or dictate a note. Thank-you notes don't have to be just for gifts.

7. Begin the magical tradition of a "thank-you fairy," who leaves little goodies and notes for jobs well done.

8. Go the extra mile to thank the people in your life—from the dry-cleaning lady to the guy who bags your groceries. Your kids are watching.

9. Be thankful for your friends and let them know how you feel. Ask your kids to come up with specific ways to appreciate and acknowledge their friends.

10. Thank God right out loud when you are moved to do so. "Thank you God for this glorious morning."

SOULFUL GIFTS

As November wraps itself around us, let's take a deep breath, pour a cup of steaming tea, and take a moment to ponder the upcoming season of holidays and festivities.

Do you feel a tightening in your throat and a trembling in your hands at the thought of shopping, cooking, planning, traveling, wrapping, visiting, wanting, scheduling? Take another sip of tea and vow that this year the holidays *will* be different. Why? Because you are beginning now. You and your family have a choice and you can choose today how to fill your calendar in the next few weeks. Schedule days for your family to be together. Decide what activities have meant something to you in the past and make room for those in your planning. Think about gifts now rather than waiting until the last minute. Gift giving doesn't have to put you in debt or take a lot of time. By planning early, you can create soulful gifts instead of frantically accumulating more plastic toys that lie abandoned in the basement. Take some time to reflect on the person to whom you are giving and the grace of soulful gifting begins.

Is there a gift you received as a child that still stays with you somehow? My grandfather gave me a few of his well-used sailing books when I was eleven. I had an interest in sailing and it touched me deeply that he would pass along his treasured books. I felt very grown-up and important because my interests were being honored.

A friend of mine spent a few hours at her local Goodwill selecting colorful dresses, hats, and shoes to fill a dress-up box for her six-year-old daughter. She asked friends and family to sort through their costume jewelry and send any cast-offs her way, and she even took in a yard sale or two. This busy mom got out a glue stick and attached glitter and plastic gems to a large cardboard trunk, which became her daughter's magical Christmas gift. Her daughter was enchanted.

How about giving your child something that means a lot to you? Your grandmother's photo in a new frame with a note attached to the back that reads, "You look so much like your great-grandmother, I wanted you to have this photo of her to remind you of your strong roots."

When my daughter was eight I gave her a little heart-shaped box with scraps of folded paper inside. On the outside of the box it said:

"Dear Elizabeth, This is an Idea Box for those times when you have nothing to do. Just reach in the heart and grab an idea or two. It's magic, you'll see—always full of notes delivered by me."

She has loved this box and goes to it often to prompt her imagination. Some of the ideas typed on slips of paper are:

- Get out all of your musical instruments and tape record some neat sound effects.
- Create your own stationery designs on the computer.
- Draw a cartoon strip using two very different characters. One is freckled and frilly: the other whittles and whistles a lot. What happens when they find a stray dog?

Have fun recalling soulful gifts you've received and planning your own gifts from the heart. Now, enjoy your cup of tea.

B A L A N C I N G   T I P S

⌐ Schedule a Saturday afternoon to gather as a family and create gifts together. Put some cider on the stove, festive music on the CD player, and roll beeswax into candles. Maybe you'd like to make inexpensive lavender sachets by stitching dried lavender into tiny pillows or let your child decorate glass bottles with nontoxic, waterproof markers. Pour in some olive oil, sprinkle in dried herbs, and you have a fun kitchen gift. This year my daughters designed fabulous stationery as gifts by decorating rice paper with rubber stamps. They also created pins and earrings using sea glass gathered over the summer.

⌐∽ Is there a particular spiritual book that has touched your soul? If so, consider contacting the author and giving a signed copy to everyone on your holiday gift list. Authors are usually thrilled to personalize books, recipients are touched by the gesture, your shopping woes are over, and you've contributed to a message that will ripple out into the world. One year I sent a favorite angel book to many friends. The author not only personalized each copy, but sprinkled angel confetti in the pages.

True gifts spring spontaneously from one's pure compassionate heart with no thought of any return.

—BUDDHA

YOU'VE BEEN THANKED

We all love to be surprised, no matter our age. It's especially wonderful to be singled out and surprised by a secret admirer. When I was a little girl, we used to leave baskets of flowers on neighbors' doorsteps each May Day and then run away. I loved the thrill of giving anonymously and the excitement of not being caught.

This year I've used Thanksgiving as an opportunity for my children to secretly thank neighbors and friends. It didn't take more than an hour, and I think we may have begun a new tradition.

If you want to join our "You've been thanked" game, here's the plan—type or write the following in the middle of a piece of paper in huge letters: I'VE BEEN THANKED!! Then draw or print from the computer an image of Thanksgiving—a turkey or a cornucopia. Now put together a little goodie bag or basket of treats—minimuffins, cookies, pumpkin bread, or even fresh fruit. The idea isn't to make yourself crazy with baking but to express thanks by giving. Write or type a little note to tuck into the basket that says something like this:

You've been thanked today for being such a great neighbor (friend) (person). Have a wonderful Thanksgiving and always remember that someone is grateful for you. Make two copies of the I'VE BEEN THANKED sign and leave the original on your front door. Now pass along a secret thank you to two others. Include the I'VE BEEN THANKED sign in each goodie bag.

Just as the sun goes down, set out to drop off your secret goodies. Bring a roll of tape to hang the sign on your unsuspecting neighbor's front door. Remember to tape up the sign, drop off the goodies, ring the bell, then run like crazy. Your children will delight in this Thanksgiving chain.

Have fun watching as your neighborhood or apartment building fills with front doors wearing the I'VE BEEN THANKED sign.

And P.S., now that our cover's blown, we might have to come up with another kind of Thanksgiving surprise!

I would maintain that thanks are the highest form of thought, and that gratitude is happiness doubled by wonder.

—GILBERT KEITH CHESTERTON

COMPASSIONATE KIDS

My daughter's class took a field trip to Boston's holocaust memorial. With tears in her eyes, Elizabeth reacted to her experience, "It was the most powerful and disturbing day in my life. Reading the words, seeing the people's numbers carved on the glass, just being there made it so real." She went on to say she had found a stone and gently placed it at the base of the memorial as her way to honor the dead.

Children feel deeply and have great compassion. Sadly, it's often we, their parents, who slowly disengage them from their caring. "It's just a story," we tell them, or, "Don't cry, it happened a long time ago." Their strong sense of empathy, however, can change the world.

What does your child care about? What grabs at *your* heart? Raising compassionate kids doesn't mean we must grumpily cram "good deeds" into a crowded schedule. Open your awareness this week to the world around you and share that awareness with your child. "That little boy dropped his ice-cream cone on the ground. He must feel really disappointed. How would you feel?" And with your older children, "My heart is heavy tonight as I read about the suffering in the world. Here's an address where we can send clothing for children. Any ideas on how we might collect more than just our out-grown clothes?"

BALANCING TIP

—᷉ Pick books to read with your young children that will ignite discussion about the feelings of others. For older kids select chapter books such as Lois Lowry's *Number the Stars*. Set aside time to read together and discuss what you've read.

—᷉ Support your child as she is inspired with ideas of actions to take that make a difference. Taking a walk with an elderly neighbor or cleaning up neighborhood litter makes a difference. Discuss the possibility of donating a toy to an underprivileged child during the holidays or a warm coat if you live in a cold climate. Depending upon your child's age, she could also volunteer at a nursing home, hospital, or soup kitchen. Linking your child's kind actions with her interests becomes a positive experience for everyone involved. A ten-year-old friend of ours plays her flute once a month at a local nursing home. She loves to perform and the residents look forward to observing her progress with each visit.

—☙ Decide that just for today you and your child will try to embrace everything you do with a higher level of compassion. Playing at recess, running a meeting, passing the peas, kicking a soccer ball will take on a new focus.

> *Each day God fills up your heart with love to give to people.*
>
> —AGE 6

COZY CONNECTEDNESS

According to author Georgia Heard, the Spanish word *querencia* describes a place where one feels safe, a place from which one's strength of character is drawn, a place where one feels at home.

Where is that place for you? Does being out in nature provide you with a rooted connection or is it under the duvet in your cozy safe bed? Maybe it's your childhood home, and you feel *querencia* when you return to visit your aging parents. Perhaps, like a friend of mine, you feel most at home in the warmth—lying on a sun-soaked rock or working in front of a sunny window.

What is your child's *querencia?* Where does he go when he's sleepy, had a bad day, wants to be alone? Is your child most often outdoors in a tree house or tucked next to you in the big, green kitchen chair?

Don't you find that your comfort level is also affected by what you are wearing? We all need clothing that lulls us to a secure, comfortable place. A pair of fleece pants with a loose elastic waist and a baggy top do it for me. I also find myself reaching for a soft, green, cable-knit sweater my grandmother made for my mother over thirty years ago. Wearing it is like being held in a warm hug. A cotton, oatmeal-colored cardigan was wrapped around my daughter's waist for the first three months of school—every day. Her *querencia?*

Open your awareness to *querencia* and link with it when you need a dose of cozy connectedness. When you're out of sorts and feeling frazzled, you might kick off your work heels and slip into scruffy slippers. When your twelve year old is looking a little dejected, guide her to the hammock where you've seen her swing away tears time after time. And when you have to be away from your baby, dress him in the softest footie jammies and leave him a shirt of yours to cuddle with—it smells just like you.

B A L A N C I N G   T I P

Become aware of the elements that support and sustain you and your children in feeling safe. A toddler's worn blankie is an obvious example. What's your blankie? How about your teenager's?

It's just a little scrap of material now but it once was a beautiful dress on my favorite doll. It was my mom's doll, too, when she was little and it meant a lot to me. I'm too big for the doll, and she's wearing a new dress now, but I sometimes tuck that little checkered piece of doll dress in my pocket when I go to school. It sorta feels like my mom, my doll, and my snugly room are going with me.

—AGE 7

PLANNING HOLIDAYS NOW

As we ease into November, let's turn our thoughts to the upcoming holiday season. Relax, I'm not suggesting you buy into the hype and frenzy that can grab us by the guilt cord and insist we unpack the little white lights the day after Thanksgiving.

Breathe deeply now

I'm encouraging you to plan now for the holiday season you intend for your family to experience. A few small actions this far in advance can truly make a difference between a sacred, intimate time of year or the last-minute frenzy we might have experienced in the past.

Here are some ideas to pave the way for a soulful, love-filled, family holiday without exhaustion:

BALANCING TIPS

—◌ Call a family meeting, or simply gather with your family over a meal, and discuss what is most meaningful to each member during the holiday season. I discovered that one child cares more about a houseful of friends and family then going out to an event. Her sister cherishes decorating the Christmas tree with our family. There's usually a fire blazing and music playing, and we share the story of each ornament as it's unpacked from the Christmas box. Guess I don't have to book *Nutcracker* tickets.

—◌ Is there a new tradition or ritual you would like to begin this year? Take a few moments and ponder what was most meaningful to you as a child. How might you begin it with your family?

—◌ Encourage family spirit by creating opportunities and rituals for sibling collaboration. Maybe the kids are in charge of planning a party for their friends at your home, making secret gifts as a team, or concocting a festive breakfast menu.

—◌ How might your family give to others from the heart? Is there a way you can reach out in your community this year? Ask your priest, rabbi, school principal, or local Head Start if they know of a particular family that is in need. Find out the ages of their children and, with yours, create a holiday box full of prizes to be delivered anonymously. There are many families outside the "system" whose spirits would be lifted by your generosity and creativity.

—⌐ Bake some cookies now and freeze them for the inevitable "bring a batch of cookies" invitation in December.

—⌐ Make sure you schedule time to experience the true spiritual meaning of the holiday. If you are part of a church or temple, hinge your celebrations around special holiday services. Find out the dates now so your calendar reflects your priorities.

—⌐ During the holidays, our self-worth can become tied up with how our family appears to others. Shift from that ego-based way of being and make plans to add depth to this year's celebrations in ways that honor much more than mere outer appearances.

Come up with ways to demonstrate to your children that:

1. Happiness is not about what we have, who we hang out with, what we do for a living, what parties we are invited to, or what we look like, but who we are deep inside, what we care passionately about, and how we spread the light of kindness in our family and in our world.

2. Giving, sharing, and forgiving are truly more rewarding than taking, accumulating, and avenging.

3. We can't control the world out there, but we have total control over our own thoughts, actions, and connection with spirit.

So get out your calendars, brainstorm with your family, phone dear friends to reserve time to be together. Plan, prioritize, and become proactive now so there is meaning and true fulfillment rather than disappointment, debt, and disgruntlement come January 1.

The afterthought is good, but forethought is better.

—NORWEGIAN PROVERB

To be prepared is to have no anxiety.

—KOREAN PROVERB

REFLECTIONS OF THE LIGHT

We are filled with a Divine essence, a soul, a spiritual core—this is who we truly are. Young children are a more pure channel for this expression because they haven't picked up the many filters we, who have lived longer, have accumulated. These filters, such as fear, suspicion, anger, guilt, and old programming, block our pure potential from manifesting as our experience.

Let's remain alert to any limiting beliefs we may be passing on to our kids. Have they heard you say, "I'm just unlucky," "Suffering is somehow holy," "I have a weak constitution," "You're moody just like your Uncle George," "Self-care is not okay," "You can't have it all?"

As your child grows older, remind her that she was created in the image and likeness of God, then talk about what that image is—pure joy, abundance, perfect health, fulfillment, peace. Is that what her experience of life is? If not, she is like most of us, living at half speed. Just like the powerful computers on our desks, we only use a portion of our enormous capacity.

Begin to identify the filters you may have accumulated, then set the intention to release them. This will create openings for your true magnificent self to shine through and miracles, coincidences, and good luck to occur.

Send limiting thoughts and useless blocks to the Recycle Bin just as routinely as you clear obsolete data from the hard drive of your computer.

BALANCING TIP

⟶ Get quiet and turn toward the light within. Picture it as the core of your being, radiating in your solar plexus, then filling your body and cocooning all around you. You are glowing with pure light. As your hand stretches out, it is encased in light. As the light surrounds your mind, what limiting thoughts might it heal? What filters are diffusing your passion, abundance, patience, full expression of creativity? See these filters being lifted up and away by the light. Now tune into your beloved child. Has he somehow picked up the same blocks? What might be limiting his experience? Notice any thoughts or insights that come to you now and throughout the week.

If we did all the things we are capable of doing, we would astound ourselves.

—THOMAS EDISON

12

DECEMBER

CREATE A SIMPLER, MORE
MEANINGFUL HOLIDAY

It's up to you either to create a holiday filled with joy and memories for your kids or anxiety and a blown budget. I'm right there with you thinking I don't have enough "stuff" for my children, feeling guilty as each festive holiday card arrives in our mailbox (we aren't sending cards this year), and wondering if we'll ever hang the little white outdoor lights.

But in the midst of all the gala events, it is truly the simple things my kids request: the ritual of opening an Advent calendar, reading a different holiday book each chilly December morning, cutting out snowflakes for the windows, making minigingerbread houses out of graham crackers, gathering old toys and books to pass along to others. Take a moment to ask yourself what the upcoming holidays mean to you and how you can make that meaning have spiritual resonance with your family?

I hope that one of the following ideas sparks a light in your heart this holiday season:

• Begin your own family traditions and let go of those that no longer move you. Perhaps you could make decorating the Christmas tree a soulful event. Play music, put some cider on the stove to warm, and let the answering machine pick up calls. When you string the lights, talk about the power of light in your lives and how we are each beacons of God's light in the world. When the light cord becomes tangled and you're about to lose control, take a deep breath, have a sip of cider, and begin again. Remember, play and enjoy the process, and you'll all cherish the end result—no matter what it looks like. You might even roll out your sleeping bags and sleep snuggled under the newly decorated tree.

• Don't forget the critters. Make ornaments for the birds using pine cones, peanut butter, and bird seed. Leave a few carrots for the bunnies, a salt lick for the deer. There's an old legend that says you can communicate with animals at midnight on Christmas Eve. When I was a young girl living in the North, my family trundled through knee-deep snow to visit with our horses in the barn, hoping to hear a few words. Ask your kids how they might give to the animals this year. Follow through on their suggestions.

• Encourage your kids to give themselves a gift this Christmas by setting a personal goal: rereading their favorite holiday book or soaking in a long, hot bath with red and green candles lighting the room. Self-care begins even with our youngest spirits.

• Turn ordinary windows into magical stained glass with pieces of colored tissue paper—tape the pieces into a collage on the glass. Suddenly your home becomes a shrine.

• Give your child a string of little white lights and let her decorate her room with them. They can stay up year-round to add magic to the ordinary.

• If you attend a particular church or temple, arrange to take your child there when there is no service. In the quiet, sacred space talk about how it feels to be there, explain the symbols, talk about the upcoming holiday and its significance. Hold hands and feel the energy of those who have prayed in this holy place before you.

• Focus on the presence not the presents.

• Eat breakfast and dinner by candlelight during the month of

December. Many Christians light weekly Advent candles symbolizing hope, peace, joy, and love. Perhaps you could discuss each quality while lighting the candle it symbolizes. Or your family might give four candles different meanings. They could represent the light of God that surrounds us, the love of God that enfolds us, the power of God that protects us, the presence of God that watches over us. As you light the new candle on Sunday, discuss what it means with your children. Create a ceremony out of the simple act of lighting a candle. Your children will delight in the event, no matter their age or their level of sarcasm, when they sense your commitment to the idea.

• Save all those wonderful family photographs you receive in holiday cards. Come January 1, bring out one photo a day and place it in the center of your kitchen table or in any central place. Bring your attention to the people pictured. A photo a day, surrounded by your prayers for their peace and joy in the new year, will deliver much more than simple good cheer back to the sender. One mom I know bundles her annual holiday cards—tying them with a beautiful ribbon. The following holiday season she rereads each one with her kids. She has about five years worth tucked away in a special box.

• Release the struggle of creating "the Perfect Holiday." Choose to let go of the things that drag you down. Who needs a fancy dinner with all the trimmings this year? Instead, make a feast out of leftovers or order take-out. The atmosphere of joy and ease is what your kids will remember.

> *I don't turn on the television set during the holidays. All the stuff on TV makes me anxious about what I might have forgotten or didn't buy.*
>
> —MOTHER OF ONE

CREATIVE RISKS

Real creativity requires us to release our tight grip of control and over-come our fear of change. Creativity can alter our lives and catapult us into a world we begin to see differently. Opening ourselves to new ideas is often the charge we need to rebalance a life that has become status quo.

Fast Company Magazine interviewed Madeleine L'Engle, author of over forty works including the classic *A Wrinkle in Time,* for their April 2000 issue. L'Engle says this about creativity: "Human beings are born with a great deal of creativity, and by the age of twelve, we've lost most of it. The world just slams it out of us. Our teachers and parents tell us what comes from our imagination isn't true; it's just 'imaginary.' I think that what's imaginary is truer than what's 'real.' Adults prefer facts, because facts are limited. Like truth, imagination is unlimited, so many people are afraid of it."

Imagination and risk are partners in an intricate, delicate, stunning dance that spins miracles into our lives. As we venture into a search for alternatives, let's encourage our children's imagination to grow, expand, and fly with their spirits—rather than wither with fear as L'Engle describes. Let's vow to resuscitate their gifts when the world "out there" holds up the blanket to smother them. As kids yearn for their parent's approval, let's applaud their deep experiment in self-expression so their strong, natural, creative ability flourishes.

Walt Whitman urged his readers to, "Bring the muse into the kitchen . . ." When we set out to support our child's creative spirit and our own, no part of our lives together is left untouched. Indeed, cook-ing soup can be a spiritual, creative, expression. I want my children to be able to activate their imaginations in their everyday lives. I want them to know themselves as the true artists they are rather than our culture's definition of an artist as a "special" person who has paintings hung in a gallery. I crave the courage to continually change the way I think, in all areas of my life.

The English word "creative" comes from the Latin *creare* meaning "to cause to grow; to bring forth, create, or produce." Isn't that what we do when we give birth to these beloved children? We till the soil of their young lives so they may flourish.

To follow are some ways you might nurture creativity in your household:

BALANCING TIPS

— It's tough to stop controlling our kids. But when we do, in a safe atmosphere of course, there is room for creative impulses. Let's manage our parenting fears so that they don't intrude on our child's imaginative expression of life. By confronting our fears we will also free ourselves to explore new territory.

— Recently my daughter was asked to fill in a map of the United States using blue ink. She raised her hand to ask, "Why must the ink be blue?" The gist of the teacher's response was, "Because I said so and you're out of line for asking." We need to encourage our kids to ask questions—good ideas often originate from curiosity. What is the question of the week your child would like to pose? Maybe this occurs at mealtimes, is posted on the fridge, or is written down in a family journal. How do you set about helping your child find answers to the question? What are stars made of? When did kneeling in prayer begin and why? What does a snowflake taste like? How are phones put together?

—⌒ Innovation comes with the belief that we as individuals are important and our ideas make a difference. Help your kids understand that they have a place in this world and a reason for being—that life is a journey of discovering our gifts and recognizing how those gifts will affect the world in a new and unique way.

—⌒ Creativity is about taking risks. Support and encourage your kids to take healthy risks even if you are risk adverse. Remember you weren't always that way. What happened to make you hide your art? Did you stop singing because you were told you had a lousy voice? Tell these stories to your kids and pick up the crayon to try again or sing out loud while making dinner.

—⌒ Faith Ringgold, who was awarded the Caldecott Medal for her illustrations in the children's book *Tar Beach,* says, "Creativity comes from our earliest desire to play." Does your child have enough time to play? To have fun, laugh, and fool around—no matter their age. Do you?

—⌒ Making fun of people, putting people down, and judging others is the surest way to stamp out creativity. Why would a child take a risk and try something "out of the box" when those who do are criticizied in your household?

—⌒ All the rules we feel are so important to raising a child who can fit into society might be blocking the next Picasso. An actress friend of mine says, "I grew up in the South of the 1950s. I've battled strong childhood programming about what is and isn't ladylike when I'm playing a part. It was tougher to lose those old scripts than my southern accent." Manners are important, they show we respect one another, but don't let "standing on ceremony" interfere with following that intuitive spark of creativity. I saw a bumper sticker recently that said, "Well-behaved girls rarely make history." Although my daughter's friend interpreted this as, "Let's go crazy and break all the rules," I happily shared my translation, "Many people try to fit into roles they feel they have to play rather than being who they are. Women who have made it into history textbooks have taken risks, spoken up, and fulfilled their dreams rather than remaining silent in the corner doing what they are told."

—❧ There is a creative power alive in the universe and we are one with that power. Spirit creates through us. How might we keep that vessel open—for our kids and ourselves?

> *To live a creative life, we must lose our fear of being wrong.*
>
> —JOSEPH CHILTON PEARCE

WINDING DOWN

It's tough to "wind down" during this festive yet frenzied stretch of days. Kids are saturated with excitement.

"Relaxation remedies" that suit your child's temperament are helpful all year long but are especially important during the holidays. I'm finding them essential these past few nights. Elizabeth is in a production of *Oliver*, which opens soon. She comes home from rehearsal full of adrenaline.

"Mom, I soak up all the energy of the other cast members." She loves it, she's high as a kite, so it takes some doing to soothe her into sleep.

All of us, no matter our age, can use the following ideas to make the transition into a restful sleep.

B A L A N C I N G   T I P S

⎯☙ A cup of warm tea can be just the tonic for letting go. Sleepy-time, by Celestial Seasonings, and any chamomile blend work like a charm for my children. I love High Lullaby by Alvita Herbal Remeteas. A sixteen-year-old friend swears it calmed her into a deep sleep before her big biology test. This tea, however, isn't recommended for kids under sixteen.

⎯☙ The bathtub can be a salvation for your fussy toddler or anxious adolescent. A hot bath is my signal that the day has ended and I can relax, so it's no surprise that my kids run a bath anytime they need to "feel better." This summer, Whitney and I discovered an incredibly relaxing bath product at Lush, a memorable store in London. It is called Bath Ballistics, and for an extravagant bath-time treat these balls of herbs, oils, and other goodies knock us out. Our favorite is Ickle Baby Baff Ballistic, and the blend of calming ingredients does the trick. If you can't find your own Bath Ballistic, try drops of aromatic herbal oil. Lavender is a sure remedy for relaxation.

⎯☙ Some kids love to be massaged at night and even a five-minute foot rub can help them release tension from the day. Give your child this exquisite gift of touch if he so desires. Clear your mind and be fully present. Sit next to his bed and pretend your hands are full of soothing, warm light that seeps into his body.

—෧ A sound machine may be just the remedy for a restless sleeper. The lull of ocean waves or pitter-patter of rainfall offers a rhythmic sound to soothe weary kids into a deep sleep.

—෧ I have grown dependent on my flax- and lavender-filled eye pillow, and woe is me if I forget it while traveling.

—෧ Help your children get in the habit of reading in bed. Somehow focusing our attention away from our lives and into a story leads many of us to slumber.

—෧ Keep the bedtime rituals to a minimum for young children. A story, a simple prayer, a kiss is just fine. When the evening dance becomes complicated, you will begin to resent it rather than looking forward to a sweet, simple time with your baby.

—෧ I tried all of the above tips the other night and Elizabeth still popped her head, full of churning thoughts, off the pillow and called to me, "Oh, Mom, I forgot to tell you the funniest thing that happened at rehearsal tonight." I didn't give up even though I wanted to squeal at her, "You've got to go to sleep or you'll be a wreck tomorrow." Here's what finally worked. "Okay, Elizabeth," I began, "picture a huge blackboard where all your thoughts are written in chalk. Now start in the upper left-hand corner and, with a clean eraser, slowly start to erase the thoughts. When the blackboard is erased, take a wet sponge and sponge it down. By the time the board is clean and dry, you will be asleep." And she was.

ANGELS

The little sandy-haired boy cradled a shoe box in his arms. He had decorated the box with glitter designs using shimmering markers and sparkly jewels. I was visiting his first-grade class to lead an angel workshop, and he had come to school with bright eyes and his precious box.

Before I had a chance to lead the children in a relaxation journey, the eager boy tugged on my sleeve. "Can I show you something, Angel Lady?" he whispered. Before the tall, imposing teacher had a chance to order the boy back to his desk, he moved in closer with his box. "Well, actually I want to tell you something first, then I'll show you this." He placed the box carefully on my lap and, looking right into my eyes, calmly as if no one else were in the room, he said, "Before my uncle died of AIDS, he told me that he would always be with me—that he would be an angel watching over me. He said that I would know he was around because I would find a feather from his wings. I looked and looked for feathers in the snow for lots of days and couldn't find my uncle's sign. Last night I found one right on my pillow." He opened the lid of the decorated shoe box to reveal a large, white feather. "I made my angel box this morning as soon as I woke up so it will always be safe."

I've had the glorious opportunity to work with many, many children, but this little boy's open, trusting spirit continues to live with me. Children and angels have a magical connection, and their angels are as vibrant and varied as the children themselves. Kids don't have to be convinced that angels exist; they know and they see. Grown-ups tend to believe that angels are merely by-products of active imaginations. Relegating angels to the world of make-believe, however, does a grave disservice to both child and adult. It denies children their rich inner lives, and it denies parents their chance to believe again.

—⃝

B A L A N C I N G   T I P S

—⃝ Ask your child to draw a picture of his angel and to describe what he draws. Write down the description on the back of the picture. Then you do the same.

—⃝ When your child has a tough time falling asleep, lead him in a soothing, guided journey to visit with his angel. Describe a lush forest with a long, winding path. At the end of the path stands his angel waiting to say good night. Use your own imagination and storytelling skills to create this fantastic place for your young child.

—⃝ Remain on the lookout for all the earth angels in your life. Think back to the times someone appeared out of nowhere to give you directions, led your wandering child back to you, passed along a book with just the right information you needed, or opened a door when your hands were full. Chat with your children about how you, too, might be angels for others.

—⃝ When your child has a particularly anxious day ahead, remind her to call upon the power of her loving angels. One seven year old told me she asks her magnificent angel to hold her hand when she walks into her first day of school. It makes her feel less alone.

> *Parents of small children can learn a great deal about angels simply by observing.*
>
> —KAREN GOLDMAN

Angels love all of the children in the world.

—AGE 6

How many angels are there? One—who transforms our life—is plenty.

—TRADITIONAL SAYING

KID SPEAK

Tonight at dinner, Elizabeth asked if she might write something for this book. As the rest of us were finishing up the dishes, she slipped out of the room and logged onto the computer. This is what she wrote. She wanted you to hear a "kid's perspective for a change."

Elizabeth says:

The best way to encourage your kid spiritually is if you simply suggest it. If you say "I'd like you to go to your room for ten minutes to meditate" they might not make the connection with God that you're trying to encourage. You should let them feel like it was their choice. A better way would be, "Would you like to take some time to talk with God today?" If your kid says "Not today" then maybe you should wait and try to do it together. If you feel like your child is having trouble understanding or doesn't seem interested, then when you think it is a good time, have a talk with him and explain why you like to pray. How do you feel close to God? Try to start a conversation. The following tips will help to encourage prayer:

- Try to pray at meal time, your kids will become familiar with the routine.

- You can also talk to God with them before they go to sleep.
- Have "Pillow Talk." You can make up prayers, too.
- Before they go to school is an excellent time to encourage them.
- If they know someone who is sick or hurt, you and your kids can ask God to help them feel better.
- Read books and watch videos that have a spiritual theme. Just because a book or tape is spiritual doesn't mean it will be boring.

I hope these tips work out. Good Luck.

If we are to attain real peace in this world, we will have to begin with the children.

—GANDHI

A PARTY WITH SPIRIT

Does the very idea of giving a party send you over the edge? How about rethinking what a holiday gathering with meaning might be like? What do you want to give your guests for the short period of time they grace your home—joy, ease, relaxation, connecting with others authentically rather than on the surface? That's a whole lot more memorable and easier to craft than heartburn and hangovers. Candles everywhere create a celebratory, serene mood. Cleaning with the intention to fill your home with light instills a glow no caterer could conjure. Including your children in the preparations eases the stress of party perfection. Simple fresh foods are a welcome relief this time of year.

I wanted to gave a party for my neighbors that left everyone joyful and revitalized during a stressful time of year rather than another obligation that cut into their sleep. So I created "A Party with Spirit" and sent out invitations that Whitney designed on the computer. I hired a masseuse who set up her funky pink chair in my family room and gave shoulder massages to appreciative guests. I asked everyone to bring a gift to swap that soothes the body, mind, or spirit. You've never seen such excited grown-ups gathered under the tree, opening candles, CDs, eye pillows, herbal wraps, meaningful books, luscious bath beads.

My neighbors, most of them harried moms, are still talking about how cared for they felt. Anyone can hang colored lights, buy exotic liquor, and arrange giant pink shrimp in a bowl. But those of us striving to live balanced, authentic lives realize it takes less time and is a whole lot more meaningful to craft a celebration with friends from the heart.

You're Invited to

SOOTHE YOUR SPIRIT
THIS BUSY HOLIDAY SEASON

Please Come to *a Gathering of*
Neighborhood Friends

Take time out from all the planning, parties,
pomp, pies, and partners to renew YOU!

WHEN:

December 17th
7:00 P.M.

WHERE:

Mimi Doe's home

Bring a gift that soothes your *body, mind,* or *spirit* to swap
(a favorite book, bath oil, chocolate bar . . . under $15).

IT'S YOUR CHOICE

Whitney was three years old and we were sitting outside enjoying luke-
warm tea in pink plastic teacups when she said, "I picked you to be my
mom. I was an angel in heaven, and I saw you and knew you were the
mom for me." I was so relieved. If this child had picked me, then I didn't
need to be the "all knowing, all perfect mother." We were somehow in
this dance together. And truly, nine years later, I feel that Whitney is one
of my greatest teachers.

It is interesting to think, as Whitney did, that we had some choice in
our current lives, that we somehow signed up for this group of individuals we call a family—challenges and all. And if we made the courageous choice to live this life, then we can choose how it unfolds from
this moment on. We can relax a little and enjoy the journey.

Begin again, right now, envisioning the life you choose to lead. How
do you want your career and family to weave together? How does your
typical day unfold? What is the essence of what you hold as dear and
important? What would you like to let go of that is holding you back
from utter happiness? How might you begin letting go? What do you
most want your children to feel when they are thirty and someone asks
them to describe their childhoods?

You don't have to have all the answers; it's not possible. In fact, it's quite delightful when your children begin to fill in the blanks for you. Let yourself off the hook for any past mistakes and make a commitment to choose consciously from this day on.

Here is a magical chant to say when you need a nudge toward making a clear choice. "I choose to make the most of today and live it with joy. I choose to move forward in my life, knowing I am doing the best I can. I make all my choices with love."

> *The strongest principle of growth lies in human choice.*
>
> —GEORGE ELIOT

NEW YEAR'S EVE

What is your family doing this New Year's Eve? More and more people I talk to have decided to buck the frenzy and stay home. So unless you're planning to jet across time zones, how about creating a soulful evening with your kids?

Each New Year's Eve my family and I set a festive table, light a fire and tons of candles, uncork the sparkling cider, and hunker in to review the year gone by and plan the year ahead.

We sort through photos taken during the year, sometimes even transferring them from a tattered cardboard box to an album. It's great fun to spark our memories with snapshots and relive the year's highlights.

The children look forward to our ritual of writing down all that we'd like to let go of from the year, then throwing the paper in the fire.

We watch what we'd like to forget turn into flames and disappear. Then we write down what we'd like to manifest in the coming year. There's something magical about gathering around the kitchen table and writing by candlelight.

We tuck the papers with our wishes into an envelope, seal it with wax (the kids love that part), and put it somewhere safe until the following New Year's Eve when the seal is broken and the wishes read.

Whatever you choose to do this New Year's Eve, do it with a clear intention. Follow your heart and your deepest intuition from December 31st onward into the glorious new year. Remember you are coparenting with God and anything is possible.

BALANCING TIP

Listen to your children's ideas on how to plan a special New Year's Eve celebration. Here's what some children have to say:

> *My brothers and I are with a baby-sitter on that night so it's just the same old thing. My mom and dad go to a party and I think they kiss people at midnight.*
>
> —AGE 8

> *New Year's Eve is special because my family is together and we have a lot of fun. It's starting over, like a new notebook. I like that feeling.*
>
> —AGE 10

I like knowing that the new year kind of creeps in during the night, and when I wake up I start the day and the year with a clean slate.

—AGE 11

I complained last year that my family never did anything fun because we always celebrate New Year's Eve at home. So my parents arranged for us all to go out to a big outdoor celebration with other families, skating, a hot tub, and lots of food. It felt funny. This year, I want to go back to our boring home traditions.

—AGE 13

Resources

PART FOUR: FALL

Adult Books

Anglescribe, Mary Ellen, *Expect Miracles*. Berkeley, CA: Conari Press, 1999. Real stories about real people and the wonderful miracles that changed their lives.

————. *A Christmas Filled with Miracles*. Berkeley, CA: Conari Press, 2000. These short, uplifting Christmas stories will surely enchant you into a magical holiday mood. Read them out loud with your children—one each day of December.

Aslett, Don. *Clutter's Last Stand*. Cincinnati, Ohio: Writer's Digest Books, 1984. Parents continue to tell me that books by Don Aslett have changed their lives for the better.

————. *Clutter Free! Finally & Forever*. Pocatello, Idaho: Marsh Creek Press, 1995.

Biziou, Barbara. *The Joy of Family Rituals*. New York: St. Martin's Press, 2000. Sometimes it just takes someone else's imagination to ignite our own. This book will ignite yours.

Debroff, Stacy, and Marsha Feinberg. *Mom Central: The Ultimate Family Organizer*. New York: Kodansha International, 1998. My friend Stacy, a busy mother of two, created this great compilation of forms, checklists, and schedules.

242 Busy but Balanced

Doe, Mimi, and Garland Waller. *Drawing Angels Near: Children Tell of Angels in Words and Pictures.* New York: Pocket Books, 1995. A whimsical romp with the angels. From the hearts, minds, and spirits of children.

Domar, Alice D., *Self-Nurture: Learning to Care for Yourself as Effectively as You Care for Everyone Else.* New York: Viking, 2000.

Elkind, David. *The Hurried Child: Growing Up Too Fast Too Soon.* New York: Perseus Press, 1998.

Gerzon, Robert. *Finding Serenity in the Age of Anxiety.* New York: Bantam Books, 1998. This book is a true guide for achieving serenity when the world is going bonkers around you.

Goldman, Karen. *The Angel Book: A Handbook for Aspiring Angels.* New York: Simon & Schuster, 1993. A book full of resources to draw you closer to your angels.

Hoff, Benjamin. *The Tao of Pooh.* New York: Penguin Books, 1992. You're never to old for a little wisdom from Pooh.

Luhrs, Janet. *The Simple Living Guide.* New York: Broadway Books, 1997. All of these simplicity books can remind us to pull in and pare down. One mom who read several of these books told me, "Before making any decisions, small and large, I think about whether it will keep our family life 'simple' or cause unnecessary stress."

Morgenstern, Julie. *Organizing from the Inside Out.* New York: Henry Holt, 1998. Just reading this book on organization made me fell less stressed.

Ryan, M. J. *Attitudes of Gratitude: How to Give and Receive Joy Every Day of Your Life.* Berkeley, CA: Conari Press, 1999. A lovely little book that illustrates how gratitude is possible even in the toughest of times.

St. James, Elaine. *Simplify Your Life.* New York: Hyperion, 1994.

————. *Inner Simplicity.* New York: Hyperion, 1995.

————. *Simplify Your Life with Kids.* Kansas City, Kansas: Andrews McNeel Publishing, 1997.

————. *Living the Simple Life.* New York: Hyperion, 1996.

Taylor, Terry Lynn. *Messengers of Light.* Tiburon, CA: HJ Kramer, 1990. One of the first angel books to spark what has become an angel movement.

Witkin, Georgia. *KidStress: What It Is, How It Feels, How to Help.* New York: Penguin, 2000.

Kids

One of the greatest resources for soulful books for children is Chinaberry Catalog. I love the descriptions as well as the reader input. Call 800-776-2242 or head over to their Web site: www.chinaberry.com.

Dahlstrom, Lorraine M. *Doing the Days.* Minneapolis, MN: Free Spirit Publishing, 1998. Get your kids writing rather than just E-mailing.

Henry, O. *The Gift of the Magi.* New York: Dover, 1992. Introduce your children to this classic book on the true meaning of giving.

Johnson, Spencer. *The Precious Present.* New York: Doubleday, 1984. This parable is for the entire family.

Packard, Gwen. *Coping with Stress.* Minneapolis, MN: Hazelden/Rosen, 1997. Basic advice for teens about handling stress.

Rosen, Michael. *Elijah's Angel: A Story for Chanukah and Christmas.* New York: Harcourt Brace, 1997. A beautiful holiday story to be read again and again. I can envision a vivid television special made from this story.

Music

Play these serene CDs in the morning rather than blasting television news:

Dan Gibson's Solitudes—Great Lakes Suite

Randall Leonard—Terra Angelica

Acknowledgments

How blessed I am to have such a supportive and loving family. My children, Whitney and Elizabeth, continue to be my teachers, inspiration, and great joy in life. I thank you both for allowing me to share snapshots of our life together. What a great thrill it is to be journeying with you two bright lights. My dear husband, Tom, knows the fine art of tolerance and has lovingly supported and encouraged me in all I do—I am so very grateful. My mother, Marsha Walch, has been an extraordinary model for me in her ability to listen authentically, lovingly mother four children, and courageously handle life's unexpected twists. I cherish our adult friendship.

Special thanks go to my delightful editor Lara Asher, whose energy and enthusiasm are a gift, and to Heather Jackson Silverman for continuing the project with her expertise. Amye Dyer is an agent extraordinare who gently guides my projects to fruition. Thank you, Amye.

Many thanks to Wendy Schuman at Beliefnet, where versions of the following thoughts originally appeared: Helping Kids Manage Fear, Strengthening Sibling Ties, Raising Children in an E-mail World, and Create a Simpler, More Meaningful Holiday.

To all the parents I have met through my workshops and talks as well as through my newsletters, I thank you for your desire to parent in a mindful way. I am so grateful for the stories you have shared, the hopes you have described, and the challenges you so squarely meet and handle day in and day out. You are all my inspiration.

About the Author

Mimi Doe is the author of *10 Principles for Spiritual Parenting: Nurturing Your Child's Soul,* which won the 1998 Parents' Choice Seal of Approval and was a finalist in the Books for a Better Life Award. *Ladies' Home Journal* called Mimi "a parenting guru," and her work has been covered in publications such as *Child, Parenting, McCall's, Family Circle, Publishers Weekly,* and *USA Today.* She has appeared on talk radio and television programs including *Oprah, Lifetime, Pax TV, Talk America, Voice of America,* and *WISDOM Radio.* Mimi is the coauthor of *Drawing Angels Near: Children Tell of Angels in Words and Pictures* and holds a master's degree in education from Harvard. Mimi's workshops and seminars have changed the way thousands of parents interact with the children in their lives. Her popular on-line newsletter has subscribers from around the world. Mimi lives with her husband and two children outside of Boston, Massachusetts.

FOR FURTHER INFORMATION:

To contact Mimi about her workshops, talks, retreats, or consulting, write or call:

Mimi Doe
Busy but Balanced
P.O. Box 157
Concord, MA 01742
Mimi@SpiritualParenting.com

Mimi would love to hear from you about your search for balance. What tips do you have for creating an active life in the world "out there" while maintaining a soulful secure life at home? To subscribe to Mimi's free on-line newsletter, go to: **www.SpiritualParenting.com.**